2004 POETRY

ONCE UPON A RHYME

IMAGINATION FOR A NEW GENERATION

Lincolnshire
Edited by Steph Park-Pirie

Young Writers

First published in Great Britain in 2004 by:
Young Writers
Remus House
Coltsfoot Drive
Peterborough
PE2 9JX
Telephone: 01733 890066
Website: www.youngwriters.co.uk

All Rights Reserved

© Copyright Contributors 2004

SB ISBN 1 84460 489 6

Foreword

Young Writers was established in 1991 and has been passionately devoted to the promotion of reading and writing in children and young adults ever since. The quest continues today. Young Writers remains as committed to engendering the fostering of burgeoning poetic and literary talent as ever.

This year's Young Writers competition has proven as vibrant and dynamic as ever and we are delighted to present a showcase of the best poetry from across the UK. Each poem has been carefully selected from a wealth of *Once Upon A Rhyme* entries before ultimately being published in this, our twelfth primary school poetry series.

Once again, we have been supremely impressed by the overall high quality of the entries we have received. The imagination, energy and creativity which has gone into each young writer's entry made choosing the best poems a challenging and often difficult but ultimately hugely rewarding task - the general high standard of the work submitted amply vindicating this opportunity to bring their poetry to a larger appreciative audience.

We sincerely hope you are pleased with our final selection and that you will enjoy *Once Upon A Rhyme Lincolnshire* for many years to come.

Contents

    Gordon Hooper (10)   1

Ancaster CE Primary School
    Ben Streeter (9)   1
    Grace Richardson (9)   2
    Emily Lord (8)   2
    Rebecca Hogben (8)   3
    Jack Corah (10)   3
    Jake Cattell (9)   4
    Ellie Talton (8)   4

Carlton Road Primary School
    Aiden Louth (10)   4
    Keith Hunter (10)   4

Denton CE School
    Sam Whaler (8)   5
    Daniella Crossland (7)   5
    Jordan Marsh (9)   5
    Emily Bennett (8)   6
    Olivia Capewell (8)   6
    Kiri Meadows (7)   7
    Luke Bennett (10)   7
    Shân Bagworth (9)   8
    Hannah West (7)   8
    Emily Robb (8)   8
    Harry Bell (8)   9

Donington Cowley Endowed Primary School
    Amber Simpson (8)   9
    Alice Rands (9)   10
    Jasmine Merry (10)   11
    Hannah Tudball (9)   12
    Chloe Hilton (10)   13
    Laura Robinson (9)   14
    Ryan Stevens (10)   15

Lauren Parker (8)	16
Lauren Munden (10)	16
Shannon Prudom (7)	17

Faldingworth Primary School
Shane O'Malley (10)	17
Alex Brown (11)	18
Theodora Badiali (10)	18
Rosie Forester (10)	19
William Clark (11)	19
Gemma Chambers (9)	20
Shannon Paige Westwick (9)	20
Samantha Carter (11)	21
Amy Smith (9)	21
Darren Porter (10)	22
Luke Robinson (10)	23

Gedney Church End Primary School
Rachel Payne	23
Josh Rylott (10)	24
Jade Pollard (10)	24
Bethaney Brothwell (11)	25
David Bray (10)	25
Henry Williams (8)	25
Chloe Putterill (8)	26
Laura Buddle (10)	26
Kate Pickering (10)	26
David Scott (10)	26
Bradley Brothwell (9)	27
Syndal Tinsley (9)	27
Stewart Hawes (10)	27
Thomas Sargeant (11)	28
Kieran Eady (11)	28

Grainthorpe Primary School
Thomas Cartlidge (9)	29
Dane Edwards-Wright (11)	29
Lauren Kennedy (9)	30
Laurie Kennedy (10)	30
Ben Lawrence (10)	31
Dale Patchett (9)	31

Hollie Quail (10)	32
Jake Roberts (10)	32
Ryan Bashford (9)	33
Brad-Lee Simister (11)	33
Tudor Roberts (9)	34
Belinda Bostock (11)	34
Jack Hannah (11)	35
Rebecca Crompton (9)	35
James Mumby (11)	36
Charlie McCarthy (11)	36
Sam Butler (10)	37
Charlotte Buckley (10)	37
Innes Adlard (11)	38
Daniel Rickett (9)	38
Jake French (11)	39
Lucia Willson (10)	39

Kirkby-on-Bain CE School

Laura Vallely (6)	39
Nicola Hill (11)	40
Edward Wright (9)	40
Mia Falcidia (9)	41
Sophie Brass (11)	42
Grace Lamyman (8)	42
Lucie Redwood (6)	43
Emma Lonsdale (9)	43
Amy Ball (10)	43
Lauren Hunter (10)	44
Josh Hunter (8)	44
Bernadette Hogg (8)	45
Eleanor Redwood (10)	45
Hannah Brass (8)	45
Alice McConnon (9)	46
Rosie Harris (8)	46
Callum Cheetham (8)	47

Monkshouse Primary School

Tom Fox (9)	47
Jack Nottingham (9)	48
Charles Chamberlain (10)	48
Crystal Gray (9)	49

Gareth Ellis (10)	49
Stacie Eden (11)	50
Josh Turner (10)	50
George Chandler (10)	51
Cherie Payne (9)	51
Vicky Orme (10)	52
Tegan Bates (9)	52
Nathan John Spendelow (10)	52
Lauren Morris (11)	53
Matthew Smith (10)	53
Oliver Smith (10)	53
Bethany Stinson (11)	54
Jake Worth (9)	54
Aimee Lauren Chamley (10)	54
Jasmine Smith (10)	55
Kimberley Clasby (10)	55
Jordan Fisher (9)	55
Bethany Copland (9)	56
Jake Haynes (10)	56
Joseph Foster (10)	56
Joshua Smith (10)	57
Georgia Lowe (9)	57
Eleanor Harrison (9)	58

Morton CE Primary School

Megan Thompson (8)	58
Sophie Stoyles (9)	59
Sebastian Murdoch (9)	59
Kayleigh Saunders (10)	60
Alice Green (9)	60
Jessica Schaffer (8)	61
Adam Smith (9)	61
Emma Marie Percy (10)	62
Darren Storey (10)	62
Alice Howlett (7)	63
Tara Mason (9)	63
Rebecca Born (9)	64
Abigail Howlett (9)	64
Bethany Fraser (10)	65
Eden Andres (9)	65

Jack Sheppard (8)	66
Kieran Grafton (9)	66
Ayisha Hanson (8)	67
Eleanor Farrow (10)	67
Lauren Dilley (10)	68
Gemma Dakin (9)	68
Samuel Doe (7)	69
Jamie Cotter (11)	69
Robert Mumby (10)	70
Daniel Jenkins (8)	70
Craig Turner (7)	71

New Leake Primary School

Tyler Burton (9)	71
Megan White (9)	72
Kayleigh Willoughby (10)	72
Rio Burton (10)	72

St Gilbert's CE School, Stamford

Lauren City (9)	73
Charles Dickinson (9)	73
Hannah Cattell (11)	74
Louisa Pini (11)	74
Sophie Earl (10)	75
Annie Davis (10)	75
Samantha Skippon (11)	76
Christina E Campbell (10)	77

St Helena's CE Primary School, Willoughby

Zantia Pinner (8)	77
Jack Whitmore-Finney (7)	78
Harriet Hanwell (7)	78
Amanda Dennis (8)	79
Rebecca Murray (9)	79
Alexandra Cairns (8)	80
Carly Hodson (10)	80
Christopher Hill (8)	81
Charlotte Ranshaw (7)	81
Jessica Bainbridge (7)	82

St Hugh's School, Woodhall Spa

Peter Weatherley (8)	82
Alicia Emma Stevens (8)	83
Kieran Godwin (9)	83
Caroline Elkington (7)	84
Jordan Cox (8)	84
Evie Kimsey (8)	84
Davyd Greenish (11)	85
Jacob Lawson (8)	85
Sarah Padley (8)	86
Aimee Fry (7)	86
James Riggall (7)	86
Olivia Shelbourn (8)	87
Constance Read (7)	87
Charlie Lundgren (8)	87
Zoe Furness (7)	88
Carrie Chan (10)	88
Dan Elkington (7)	88
James P Rollinson (9)	89
Victoria Elkington (10)	89
Matthew Lyon (10)	89
Peter Duncanson (10)	90
Alex Bake (10)	90
Phoebe Haller (10)	90
Sarah Richards (10)	91
Matthew Tilley (10)	91
Harriet Stovin (9)	92
Thomas Shelbourn (10)	92
Peter Watson (8)	93
Tobias Downes (8)	93
Hannah Done (8)	94
Daisie Winwright (10)	94
William Fowkes (9)	95
Alex Lawson (10)	95
Nathan Kimsey (10)	96
Felicity Greenish (11)	96
Amy Furness (9)	97
Emily O'Hara (10)	97
Antonia Caranza (11)	98
Tamara Walker (9)	98
Andrew Avison (10)	98

Matthew Stovin (10)	99
Esther Malcolm (9)	99
Mathilda Dennis (10)	99
Gemma Kimsey (9)	100
Natalie Wilderspin (9)	100
Tom Craven (9)	100
Huw Greenish (9)	101
Arthur Brown (9)	101
Daniel Hallett (9)	101
Alana Howe (9)	102
Heather Marsay (8)	102
Charlotte Hanes (8)	103
Jacqui Baxter (9)	103

Stickney CE Primary School

Chloe Slater (10)	104
Athena Pears (10)	105
Jamie Pewton (11)	106
Pamela Leigh (10)	107
Thomas Scott (10)	108
James Naylor (11)	108
Andrew Houldershaw (10)	109
Heather Guy (11)	110
Nicholas Appleyard (11)	111
Emilie Kerr (10)	112
Melissa Bett (10)	113
Natasha Corbitt (10)	114
Roxanne Lenton (11)	115
Natasha Mitchell (10)	116
Emily Dodds (10)	117
Nadine Motley (11)	118
Merrick Shaw (10)	119
Casey Jee (10)	120
Sinead Holland (11)	120
Francesca Warder (10)	121
Rosemarie Holmes (11)	122

The Earl of Dysart Primary School

Liam Greaves (9)	122
Lauren Towle (10)	123
Kayleigh Otter (10)	123

Calum McGhee (9)	124
Chaunie Dolby (9)	124
Toni Freestone (9)	125
Kirsty Collin (10)	125
Aiden Wood (10)	126
Sophie Mudie (9)	126
Jamie Lawson (9)	127
Conor Bowen (10)	127
Brandon Duffiold (9)	128
Toni Morton (10)	128
Daniel Eve (10)	129
Alex Harrold (9)	129

The Richmond School

Henry Cliffe (10)	130
Hannah Muirhead (9)	130
Grace Phelps (10)	131
Sophie Gorrick (10)	131
Bobbi Stead (10)	132
Lucie Millitt (9)	133
Jake Epton (9)	134
Rebecca Cram (9)	135
Brett Mason (10)	136
Bryony Hawkesford (10)	137
Sarah Beal (10)	138
Callum Dewar (10)	139

Tower Road Primary School

Alex Pycock (10)	140
Finn Lewis (9)	140
Sadia Aslam (9)	141
Alistair Wood (10)	141
Charlotte Doddrell (10)	142
Michael Craven (8)	142
Katie Toyne (11)	143
Lucy Doddrell (8)	143
Aidan McClure (10)	144
Mehroz Waheed (9)	144
Aafreen Shaikh (11)	145
Ella Dodd (9)	145
Joe Roper (11)	146

Hanna Zafar (9) 147
Natasha Lenton (9) 148
Lindsay Atkinson (9) 148

Weston Hills CE Primary School
Adelaide Esdale (8) 149
Demi Powell (9) 150
Kate Harwood (9) 150
Jacob Read (9) 151
Beth Turnell (9) 151
Jade Gilbert (8) 152

The Poems

Up And Down

Up and down
The world may be
But where altogether
Can't you see?

The moon is bright
As the stars in the sky
That twinkle like diamonds
Or rubies by far.

The dark is black
As black as coal
To keep us warm
Our horse and foal.

Around the corner
You might see
The children play
As happy as can be.

Gordon Hooper (10)

Snow Time

Snow comes
sparkling and fluffy,
Snow comes
in a thick coated blanket,
Snow comes
with loads of footprints,
Snow comes
with snowmen of all shapes and sizes,
Snow comes
with sledging down steep hills,
Snow comes
with snowflakes that swirl and twirl,
Snow sadly ends
with mushy, slushy slush.

Ben Streeter (9)
Ancaster CE Primary School

Snow

Snow comes
        silently like a glittering white blanket.
Snow comes
        fluttering softly down.
Snow comes
        with children barging outside.
Snow comes
        with crunching, slippy ice.
Snow comes
        bringing wet wellingtons.
Snow comes
        smoothing the ground.
Snow comes
        redecorating the land.
Snow crunches
        everywhere.

Grace Richardson (9)
Ancaster CE Primary School

Snow

Snow comes silently down like gleaming glitter
Snow comes with wrapped up children coming out to play
Snow comes and freezes the day
Snow comes with people crunching on the ice
Snow comes but the children are waiting for more snow
Snow comes with just plain white snow
Snow comes with children out to play.

Emily Lord (8)
Ancaster CE Primary School

Snow

Snow comes
        gently down to me.
Snow comes
        sparkling down.
Snow comes
        playing with me.
Snow comes
        softly down to me.
Snow comes
        fluttering down to the ground.
Snow comes
        powdery, down to me.
Snow comes
        like a lovely blanket.

Rebecca Hogben (8)
Ancaster CE Primary School

Snow

Snow comes down to Earth,
Snow comes with people wrapped up warm,
Snow comes with gentle falling snowflakes,
Snow comes with smiling little faces,
Snow comes with glittering, soft snow,
Snow comes as light as a feather,
Snow comes down with ice,
Snow comes with wet slushy stuff.

Jack Corah (10)
Ancaster CE Primary School

Snow

Snow comes and goes
Snow comes with a powdery look
Snow comes with a crunchy sound
Snow comes with a smooth touch
Snow comes and follows you
Snow comes and melts and ends.

Jake Cattell (9)
Ancaster CE Primary School

Snow

Snow comes in little white flakes.
Snow comes with me putting on my wellingtons.
Snow comes and goes the next day.
Snow comes with me in my hat and coat.
Snow comes down tenderly and weak.
Snow comes softly down.

Ellie Talton (8)
Ancaster CE Primary School

Cat Haiku

My cat is loving
My cat catches little birds
My cat's got sharp claws.

Aiden Louth (10)
Carlton Road Primary School

Monkey Haiku

Brown cheeky monkey
Swings through trees in the jungle
Eats a banana.

Keith Hunter (10)
Carlton Road Primary School

Football

Football is fun,
Football is cool,
Football is great fun, better than a pool.
You play in mud,
You play in grass,
But you never play on glass.
You play with a ball,
You play in your boots,
But it sounds like a little owl hoot.

Sam Whaler (8)
Denton CE School

My Cat Trine

She is a cuddly cat,
Trine plays with me.
She chases her string around the room.
Trine is funny,
She is black and white,
Trine purrs in front of the fire,
'Miaow, miaow, I want my food'
I love my cat Trine.

Daniella Crossland (7)
Denton CE School

Cat And The Mouse

A cat is smelling a mouse,
The mouse lives in my house,
The cat finds the mouse that lives in my house,
The cat is hungry and wants to eat,
He's looking around for some meat,
With his big cat eyes,
He can see a meat pie.

Jordan Marsh (9)
Denton CE School

My Rabbit

My rabbit is cute and cuddly,
He has a twitching nose,
My rabbit is fluffy and furry,
He likes to do a pose.

My rabbit is funny and floppy,
I love him lots and lots,
He loves his dinner all the time,
I like it when he hops.

My rabbit is very good company,
He sleeps in the sun,
When we let him out in the garden,
He goes crazy and starts to run.

Emily Bennett (8)
Denton CE School

Pip

I have a dog whose name is Pip,
A black and white cross collie,
She's very cute with pointy ears,
And always really jolly.

She likes to run so very fast,
Although she's getting quite old,
She chases rabbits, hares and squirrels,
But never catches so much as a cold!

I wouldn't be without my dog,
And love her lots and lots,
She's everything a pet should be,
And a whole lot more on top!

Olivia Capewell (8)
Denton CE School

My Sister

I have a little sister
She always drives me mad
And makes me sad.

She's funny and she's clever
She makes me laugh
She plays good games
And shares the toys she's got.

She plays with snails and worms
We argue every day
My sister's name is Kaylie
But I love her anyway.

Kiri Meadows (7)
Denton CE School

Autumn

As the setting sun dips down behind the pink clouds,
The speckled thrush sings its evening song.
The soothing wind rustles gently through the crimson trees,
Causing the crispy leaves to float slowly to the ground.

The ongoing happy cries from the children,
Opening green spiky shells to find shiny brown conkers.
The dainty fieldmouse is disturbed by the robust combine harvest
Chugging up and down every bronze filled field.

The burning smell and heat from the raging bonfire
Is too unbearable to miss.
The lovely warmth of hot dogs and tea to keep you going
Through the fantastic different colours of the blazing firework display.

I love autumn!

Luke Bennett (10)
Denton CE School

Space

Up in space it's frightening,
It starts to feel like lightning,
The stars sparkle in the night,
Although it gives spaceman a fright!

Shân Bagworth (9)
Denton CE School

Sport

N etball is good fun,
E veryone joins in,
T he game is easy to play,
B ut it can be hard to shoot,
A ny age can play,
L et's all have a
L augh!

Hannah West (7)
Denton CE School

Bikes

As I ride my bike
It shimmers in the light
I ride it through the night
And do as I like.

As I go down the hills
I pull on my brakes
My seat really kills
I nearly land in the lakes.

Emily Robb (8)
Denton CE School

My Football Team

Crusaders is the name of the team,
On the pitch, we try to act mean,
Chloe, Angus, Marcus at the back,
Harry and Fraser lead the attack,
We try to win but often lose,
But the results we cannot choose.

Harry Bell (8)
Denton CE School

Forest

Trees rapping
Arms tapping
Sprouting with golden earrings.

Birds singing
Leaves flinging
People climbing on a frame.

Trees low
Branches blow
All looking the same.

Trees sway
Every day
Armies in a row.

Crunchy frost
Leaves lost
Giraffe reaching to the clouds.

Amber Simpson (8)
Donington Cowley Endowed Primary School

Life Of A Tree

In winter, trees lose all their leaves.
When the wind is blowing, the trees
Billow out their branches.
When the breeze calms down,
The tree is as still and still as a statue
Trees become as bare as bare
During the winter season.

Springtime comes
Bursting buds explode open,
While the old summer leaves
From last year droop off the
Mossy branches.
Soon the spring buds,
Make the tree full of green colour.

Summer arrives
The trees are full of lush green leaves
The sun struggles to shine through
The trees leaves.
Summer trees bare handsome green leaves
As green as a grasshopper.

As autumn creeps towards it
The green leaves turn brown and yellow
All the leaves drop off,
Onto the thick leaf covered ground.

And then of course comes winter,
Just back in time to end the year.

Alice Rands (9)
Donington Cowley Endowed Primary School

Frosted Snowflake Tree

Snowflakes twinkle in the light
A deep black hole is starting to appear
Shadows around me, icicles twinkle
There's a star above, that shines on me
Glittery snowflakes fall in the dark
There's a howl in the wind
And a sway on me.

Old-age shadows group together
Wrinkled strips of bark are creating a body
An old-aged body
It has snowdrops that twinkle
And arms that stretch out.

Snowflakes twinkle in the light
A deep black hole is starting to appear
Shadows around me icicles twinkle
There's a star above, that shines on me
Glittery snowflakes fall in the dark
There's a howl in the wind
And a sway on me.

Wooden fingers thread together
Images of faces swiftly flow across my mind
I hear a sound
A gentle sound
Like a little bird whistling in the air.

Jasmine Merry (10)
Donington Cowley Endowed Primary School

Through The Seasons

Winter trees are bare,
With wrinkled trunks
Some tall and bald.
Sparkling branches,
From the snow,
Icicles hanging,
All around.

Spring trees are mossy,
With buds on
Tips of the branches.
The sun shines on
New buds, giving them food
All around friends are growing,
And followers being born.

Summer trees are tall,
With green leaves,
Tickling the cloud's toes.
The summer sun tries
Frantically to burst its
Golden rays through
The net of leaves.

Autumn trees are brown
With golden leaves,
Some red, some yellow
The cold autumn air blows
Crinkled leaves off the waving branches,
Falling swiftly
The leaves trickle to the green floor,
Forming a blanket of leaves.

Hannah Tudball (9)
Donington Cowley Endowed Primary School

Old Age Comes To Everything

It's amazing how such a long life is created,
From such a small seed.

Nursing the new intruder,
As it bursts its way through the solid ground,
The luscious grass comforts the young,
As lullabies are sung in the cold, windy nights.

Getting used to its environment,
Childhood is coming close,
The sapling watches in fear,
As friends and family are decaying and being taken away.

Late in adolescence,
Wise with power and strength.
Seen what happens in life,
Knowing what lies ahead.

Adulthood on its way,
Now solid and dependable,
Its wooden fingers reach out to the sky,
Protecting its loyal from danger.

Old age with its twists and turns,
Bring its turning fortune.
How long it look to get to this stage,
It dies, decays and gives food to others.
Old age comes to everything even to trees.

Chloe Hilton (10)
Donington Cowley Endowed Primary School

Family Tree

Ever since I was born
We have had a sycamore tree
It stands tall and proud
Like a watchman in front of our house.

It was there before my grandfather's grandfather
Planted and nursed by my ancestors
It's been there all my life.

It's there whatever the weather
Waiting for me to look out
When the wind whistles through the leaves
He waves at me like a friend.

In the night when the wolves howl
It's there soothing me to sleep
And in the morning when I look out
It's there smiling at me.

But last night a man climbed up
And robbed us blind
So we chopped the tree down
Helplessly it grabbed at me
I smiled and watched it go.

Laura Robinson (9)
Donington Cowley Endowed Primary School

Trees Are A Beautiful Part Of Nature

Trees look like elephants trunks,
With the rain bursting through the golden sunlight,
Trees clamber out of their soil bed
And stretch their giant wooden fingers.

As the trees sway out of the soil,
The wind helps the trees to dance,
The swirling seed from a sycamore tree
Swirls like a whirlpool in the midnight wind.

The evergreen leaves of a evergreen tree
Sway and swerve lush and green
The bark of the tree is khaki and brown
Nodulous and crumbly - but still they live.

The green leaves catch the sunlight,
In their beautiful net,
As the tree waves in the wind,
To the wonderful nature around it.

Trees are parted from their mates,
As they topple to the ground,
But at least the tree knows . . .
A new body will be born.

Ryan Stevens (10)
Donington Cowley Endowed Primary School

A Tree's Life

Winter trees bare,
Nursing their baby - cold as ice.
Like people stretching their arms out,
So much like a blob in the distance.

Evergreens take as long to grow as a snail moving.
Every tree nurses their child when they burst through.
Trees like a still, stone shadow.

All trees do is stand there - as still as a stone shadow.
All young babies standing near their mothers,
Leaves waddle like penguins skidding on the ice.

Nobody really cares about winter trees.
People like winter, but not the trees.
Children love to climb on them -
In the summer.

The tree is now one hundred years old,
It's time for it to go,
Men have come along, to chop it down,
The tree has now gone.

Lauren Parker (8)
Donington Cowley Endowed Primary School

An Old Tree

The wind whistles through tangled branches
And the sun strikes at his leaves.
He reaches out a wooden hand
And pats me on the shoulder.
He stretches his fingers into the sky
And grasps at the wispy clouds above.
They part for him,
As up he grows,
In length, age and wisdom.

Lauren Munden (10)
Donington Cowley Endowed Primary School

Trees A Tree's Life

Growing from a seed
Into a giant tree
Growing fresh leaves
Dropping delicious fruit
For you and me.

Pinky blossom covers
Like candyfloss
It must die in winter
But come back in spring.

The chopping kills a tree
It is dead for now
But a new tree will replace it
Somehow.

This tree will grow
Be strong and healthy too
It will too get cut down
Some day.

Shannon Prudom (7)
Donington Cowley Endowed Primary School

The Gold Tipped Knife

There was an abandoned cinema
On the edge of town
Which is called the
Golden Palace of Fear.
On every cloudless night
When the moon shines,
The petrifying spirits appear.
It is the spirit's playground,
A host of them waiting to come back to life,
They look like shiny balls of glittery blue light,
They can only be killed with a gold tipped knife!

Shane O'Malley (10)
Faldingworth Primary School

The Extraordinary Box

In the centre of the countryside,
A man galloped on his horse,
They got to the foretold house,
He pushed the wooden door open with a mighty force.

The house looked tarnished,
With spiders' cobwebs like the silver moon,
And squeaking mice on the floor which was varnished,
But there was still nobody there.

He thrust the door open,
In the middle of the room,
Was a shining box like a block of gold,
When he got nearer, he heard a tune.

He looked around the dingy, dusty, dirty hall
He saw no traps on the ceiling or floor
He heard no whisper or calls
He opened the box and he was no more.

Alex Brown (11)
Faldingworth Primary School

The Traveller

A traveller trots on his horse to a mysterious place,
He gets off his horse to see what's ahead.
Sees a graveyard and an old church.
Went to look around,
In the dusty, misty and silver moonlight,
Comes to the church and knocks on the door,
The door swings open, he walked inside.

Suddenly he bumps into something,
He switched on the light and looked down to
Find no feet!
Goes rushing outside on to his horse,
Gallops away with fear and never goes there again.

Theodora Badiali (10)
Faldingworth Primary School

The Wolf

A man came riding on his strong, white horse
Up a steep hill in the misty moonlight,
He jumped off his horse onto the springy grass,
And the silver watch on his wrist struck midnight,
Carefully he led his horse higher up the cliff,
The horses ears cocked and it stood statue still,
The man pulled the reins but the horse wouldn't move,
He noticed it was gazing at the top of the hill,
The man looked up and saw a ghostly wolf,
He looked away, shaking all over,
Suddenly there was an eerie howling,
The petrified horse galloped away,
Leaving its owner and the hair-raising growling
The wolf's glowing eyes stared at the man,
It howled again and he decided to run,
The wolf followed him to the edge of a village,
It quickly vanished, its work was done.

Rosie Forester (10)
Faldingworth Primary School

The Haunted Hanger

On a dark and dismal night,
A man went to explore,
The old abandoned airfield,
And found a hanger door.
He went inside the hanger,
And saw a battered plane,
Then looked around the rundown place,
He felt hot and shook with pain,
He crawled to the corner of the room,
And shed a tiny tear,
He said his life was over,
Then started to disappear.

William Clark (11)
Faldingworth Primary School

The Old School

There was an old school in the darkness,
The moon was shining bright,
Every time you went to look
You got a dreadful sight,
A boy went to have a look
He saw a woman there
He said, 'Argh somebody help me,'
'Oh don't worry, come up the stairs,'
He ran down the corridor to get out the way,
The ghost leapt on his back,
But went right through him,
Threw him in a corner it suffocated him with a sack,
The police came to the house to see what was wrong,
They climbed into the house,
They saw a shadow on the wall,
Went up to it but it was just a little mouse.

Gemma Chambers (9)
Faldingworth Primary School

The Midnight Train Track

Out in the midnight darkness,
Waiting for the late night train,
Walking down the railway path,
In the cold, wet rain,
All of a sudden, he hears a noise,
Coming from the track,
He picked up his bags and got ready to leave,
Suddenly something stabbed him in the back,
Making him fall down, down, down to the ground,
He was just lying there in despair,
The chain he was wearing twisted in the moonlight,
As he stared up in the sky he noticed misty air,
As he passed away, away, away
As he passed away.

Shannon Paige Westwick (9)
Faldingworth Primary School

The Headless Horseman

Every night across Faldingworth Hills,
When the smiling man floats in the dark night sky,
The headless horseman travels on his strong, brown, cheeky horse,
He threatens to people that they will die.

A girl appears in a window upstairs,
And decided that she wanted to investigate,
All she did was stand and stare,
She could no longer wait.

The headless horseman went riding,
Riding past the moon, moon,
In the middle of the night, night,
To kill, kill, kill!

Samantha Carter (11)
Faldingworth Primary School

Mystery Man

There was an old gravedigger
In the misty moonlight,
In a dark leather jacket,
With his socks pulled up tight,
He said, 'Farewell Earth,'
Then stepped into his grave,
'No one will see me
Until I come back again!'
After ten years it has stayed that way
But in World War III he came back,
With his leather jacket wandering the streets of London.
But this time he was wearing a rucksack,
Gun in hand he saved a woman,
Who he married and had three children with,
Abandoned her and his children
Then at the full moon, he went back to the grave with a bang
And that was the end of old man Sam.

Amy Smith (9)
Faldingworth Primary School

The Phantom

As the boy woke up he felt thirsty,
So he clambered out of bed,
But then he noticed a ghastly ghostly figure
Or was thirst playing with his head?
But then the phantom pointed down the stairs
He aimed a finger at the door,
When the little boy examined him,
The ghost didn't touch the floor,
Then the ghost beckoned,
For the boy to come near,
'Follow me' he said
And he said it loud and clear.
So the boy followed the phantom
He led him far away,
The boy got quite frightened,
He thought he would never live to see another day,
The phantom led him to the graveyard
And pointed to a stone.
He wiped off all the mucky moss
Then noticed he was alone,
The boy then read the gravestone
It read his name,
Where was he?
And what was this ghost's game?
He listened and turned around,
There stood his worst nightmare,
He tried to run
But the whole town was this thing's lair.

Darren Porter (10)
Faldingworth Primary School

The Graveyard

A man in a graveyard is filling a hole,
And a wolf howls in the street,
He looks around to find a wolf,
All his body shaking including the feet,
A bony hand pops up from the ground,
Grabs his neck, pulls him down,
He can't get up,
So he shouts to the town,
Shouting, 'There's nothing you can do now.'
The wretched delicate church just watches them fight,
The man struggles so hard,
They fight in the dark there is no light,
Everything is so, so still,
The man escapes, he runs into the church alone,
But the skeleton follows him in the dark,
The man wants to ring someone, he has no phone,
The skeleton walks in the ancient church,
It could collapse anytime now,
The skeleton slams the door,
It collapses, wow!
The man is free, he can go,
The skeleton is left there lying on the ground,
The man runs home happy as a white Christmas,
The man is now safe and sound.

Luke Robinson (10)
Faldingworth Primary School

Orange

I'm a fruit and I'm very cute,
Squidgy and juicy,
Eat me in the day,
Eat me at night,
And you will always be alright.

Rachel Payne
Gedney Church End Primary School

Tiger

People stare at them in the zoo,
Haven't got friends,
Haven't got a real home,
They can't hunt food
Zookeepers give it to them themselves,
People kill them, skin them and sell them as rugs,
People come to stare at them all day long,
And the zookeepers don't keep them warm,
I was hunting because the door was open
And for some breakfast, then I heard a noise,
It was the sound of a jeep at full speed coming to get me.
They didn't see me I thought if he is alone
He can be my breakfast,
Then I saw a head peaking in my cave,
Then as quick as a flash I pounced
With a bite, then I had some breakfast.

Josh Rylott (10)
Gedney Church End Primary School

Food Haiku

A crunchy apple,
The sour taste down my throat,
The hard, smooth apple.

The thick bananas,
Squishy yellow banana,
Massive banana.

Crunchy cucumber,
Long, thin skinned vegetable,
Crispy cucumber.

Ugly fruits are nice,
Juice runs down my cheeky chops,
Green-skinned ugly fruit.

Jade Pollard (10)
Gedney Church End Primary School

Food Haiku

Tomatoes are red,
Tomatoes are very nice,
They are very sweet.

Apples are shiny,
Sometimes they are red and green,
They are nice and sweet.

Bethaney Brothwell (11)
Gedney Church End Primary School

Blue Is . . .

A car shooting down the motorway,
A school jumper going in the wash
When I get home,
The sea crashing on the beach,
A book begging to be read,
A folder full of work ready to
Be looked at,
The sky waiting to be lit by the sun.

David Bray (10)
Gedney Church End Primary School

Green Is . . .

Grass growing in the garden,
Trees allowing the birds to nest,
Bushes blooming with bursts of flower,
Shrubs shrivelling in the hot summer sun,
Leaves leaving the lovely trees,
Goblins gobbling lots of grannies.

Henry Williams (8)
Gedney Church End Primary School

Silver Haiku

Silver glistening,
Silent, silver, sparkling stars,
Flash in the moonlight.

Chloe Putterill (8)
Gedney Church End Primary School

Gym Haiku

Gym is a good sport,
You go on bars, beam and vault,
You can do backflips.

Laura Buddle (10)
Gedney Church End Primary School

An Animal Haiku

Guinea pigs are cute,
Munching away on carrots,
Loves lots of lettuce.

Kate Pickering (10)
Gedney Church End Primary School

Haiku

Big tractors are slow,
Going down the road like snow,
Chug, chug, down the road.

David Scott (10)
Gedney Church End Primary School

Dragon Haiku

A large fierce dragon,
He would like to eat us up,
Knight came to kill him.

Bradley Brothwell (9)
Gedney Church End Primary School

Space Haiku

Zoom, zoom in the sky,
They are here saving the world,
Go around the world.

Rocket in the sky,
Bright as a lit up city,
Rockets speeding fast.

Silently, slowly,
Blue Earth speeding through the sky
Turning slowly round.

Syndal Tinsley (9)
Gedney Church End Primary School

Countries

Denmark
Denmark's red and white,
Lost 3-0 in the World Cup,
Lost against England.

England
England speaks English,
They live on a small island,
Their flag's red and white.

Stewart Hawes (10)
Gedney Church End Primary School

Country Haiku

Arctic, very cold,
The home of the blue whale
And big polar bears.

Britain, rains most days,
With badgers running away
And foxes flee fast.

Canada, wet, wet,
Timber wolves hunt day and night,
Which take down the moose.

Russia, cold as ice,
Skies watched by the sparrowhawk,
Mountains full of snow.

India, spice, spice,
Venom from the king cobra,
Stripes from the tiger.

Thomas Sargeant (11)
Gedney Church End Primary School

Tigers

I am no danger,
You may think I am,
With flesh ripping teeth,
I use them only to eat.

It's you who's *danger*
Shooting my relatives for their skin
And capturing us for zoos.

You wreck my homes and build roads
Through the forest,
You pollute them too.

If you want to save something, save me.

Kieran Eady (11)
Gedney Church End Primary School

Blue

Feeling blue,
Feeling miserable,
Very sad,
Crying faces.

Ocean blue,
Big waves,
Crashing sea,
Shiny fish.

Sky blue,
Crosses of aeroplane smoke,
Puffy clouds,
Colourful rainbow.

Jumper blue,
Happy children,
Playing noisily,
Full of laughter.

Thomas Cartlidge (9)
Grainthorpe Primary School

A New Day

It's so early in the morning,
A new day is dawning,
The birds are singing,
Like tiny bells ringing.
I stretch and yawn,
A new day is born,
I get out of bed,
I need to be fed.
It's a good day to play,
The sun is shining,
I need to be outdoors.

Dane Edwards-Wright (11)
Grainthorpe Primary School

Blue

The dragonfly glimmers,
Blue in the sky,
The dolphin swimming,
Free in the shimmering
Blue sea.
Violets so small in the
Soft green grass
The kingfisher flies
And dives into
The stream.
The blue whale emerges from
The salty sea.
Blue is for the bright sky
And for sapphires in jewellery.

Lauren Kennedy (9)
Grainthorpe Primary School

My Kitten Tiny

Cute-cuddly,
Dirty-muddy,
Cotton-wheeler,
Yummy-mealer,
Fierce-kitty,
More than witty,
Hates dogs,
Chasing frogs,
Loves food,
In the mood,
Big eater,
Fit as a cheetah,
Love sleeping,
Warm-bed keeping.

Laurie Kennedy (10)
Grainthorpe Primary School

Sweets

Twix
Two sticks,
Magic Stars
Mars.
Sweets are yummy,
I like them
So does my tummy.
Maltesers and
Snickers,
Are my favourite.
Sweets are delicious,
Sweets are yummy,
I like sweets
So does my tummy.
And if my tummy
Had no treats,
My heart would skip
A couple of beats.

Ben Lawrence (10)
Grainthorpe Primary School

Horse Kennings

Flash-canter,
Slow-walker,
Fast-eater,
No-speaker,
Mud-roller,
Mighty-sleeper,
High-jumper,
Carrot-muncher,
Country-stroller.

Dale Patchett (9)
Grainthorpe Primary School

Yellow

The sunflower stands tall, luminous,
Yellow in the sunrays,
Sun sparkling yellow in the sky,
As I pass by.
Buttercups glistening,
Yellow in the meadows,
When the sun bounces
Off my golden retriever,
Onto the grass, it lights up yellow.
The wasps have come to taste
The sweetness of the drink.
Pick some buttercups,
Fill a jar with water,
Put them in the sunlight.
Watch the hoverflies land near you,
Amazing perfection in life.

Hollie Quail (10)
Grainthorpe Primary School

Harvest Of Red

Red is for apples, juicy and sweet,
Fire gleams on a winter's night,
The farmer gathers in the cherries,
The strawberries ripen,
And the grapes grow sweeter and juicier.

The farmer picks the beetroot,
While the tomatoes grow huge.
Ladybirds eat greenflies off rose bushes,
They're the gardener's friend,
Red is the colour of the harvest.

Jake Roberts (10)
Grainthorpe Primary School

My Dog

M y pet dog Monty,
O h what a wonderful dog, he is,
N ever being good,
T rying to get upstairs,
G olden Labrador, yes he is,
O bedient, he is not,
M onty is my pet dog.
A nd he licks me all over,
R ound the garden, he runs,
Y awning as he gets tired.

D ogs are man's best friend,
O ver and over, his tail wags,
G orgeous dog, he is.

Ryan Bashford (9)
Grainthorpe Primary School

The Barn Owl

I live in a barn all alone in the night,
I look friendly but look like a ghost in the dark.
In the morning
I glide down to get my prey,
I glide very silently.
But they notice me,
So they run away from me.
They think I'm a huge, mean beast,
They are terrified of me,
It's not my fault, I'm big and scary.

Brad-Lee Simister (11)
Grainthorpe Primary School

Staffordshire Bull Terrier Acrostic

S taffordshire's are fun,
T oday my Staffordshire bathes in the sun,
A nd my Staffordshire loves me,
F antastic dogs Staffordshire's are,
F un and good to play with,
O ld-aged but loyal,
R ed-brown is my Staffordshire's colour,
D ogs are a boy's best friend,
S taffordshire's especially,
H aving fun is a Staffordshire's favourite game,
I love my Staffordshire,
R eady and waiting,
E xcellent at doing tricks.

Tudor Roberts (9)
Grainthorpe Primary School

Dogs

Meat-eater,
Long-leaper,
Midnight-creeper,
Deep-sleeper,
Long-walker,
Quick-runner,
Dog-chaser,
Ball-snatcher,
Sleep-talker,
Loud-barker,
Door-guarder,
Deep-breather,
Digging-deeper.

Belinda Bostock (11)
Grainthorpe Primary School

My Dog Rolo

My dog is as bad as a sting from a bee,
My dog always has it in for me.
He always nicks my place on the seat,
He always gives off an unusual heat.

My mum says he has the Devil in him,
He is always rummaging through the bin.
He always rips up my cousin's ted,
And then hides it in his bed.

In the morning he's never boring,
By the afternoon he is always snoring.
His teeth are baring,
When he is tearing.
My dog is as cute as can be,
But I will always remember he has it in for me.

Jack Hannah (11)
Grainthorpe Primary School

Purple

Purple is for lilac,
Sweet smelling in the garden,
Butterflies are fluttering all around,
Purple elderberries hanging from the trees,
And purple is for amethyst, the birthstone of February,
Blackberries juicy and sweet,
Around my window wisteria hangs from boughs,
The scent of lavender drifts through the air.

Rebecca Crompton (9)
Grainthorpe Primary School

Titanic

There she is, wrecked
At the bottom of the sea.
Solitude and loneliness.
She was goddess of the sea then,
Those proud days long ago,
She's had them now,
She's wrecked, lonely.
That fateful day,
The iceberg made her days end.
Now she's at the bottom
Of the cold sea.
Never to come to the top again.
She dreams in the cold silence,
Of a return to glory.

James Mumby (11)
Grainthorpe Primary School

A Pig Kennings

Mud-splasher
Food-masher
Slow-dasher
Big-boulder
Good-roller
Very round
Safe and sound
Disgusting-eater
Loud-sleeper
Chicken-chaser
Good-muncher
Ace-grunter
Straw-muddler
Farmer-cuddler.

Charlie McCarthy (11)
Grainthorpe Primary School

Red

Red is the colour of fire,
Red is for my spelling book,
Red is for the breast of the robin,
Red is for flames that are burning hot.

Red is the colour of my dad's car,
Red is the colour of my art book,
Red is the colour of my homework book,
Red is my nose when it's cold.

Red is for the ribbon on the Christmas tree,
Red is the colour of the poppies in the field.
Red is the favourite colour of mine.

Sam Butler (10)
Grainthorpe Primary School

The Deep Ocean

The fish dart across the clear blue sea,
The tidal waves crashing against the rocks,
And the tide, moving in and out.
The sun glitters on the ocean,
Seabirds surf the waves,
The deep-breathing of the ocean.
Whales surface for air, blowholes
Like living fountains,
Never-ending depths,
Of the deep blue ocean.

Charlotte Buckley (10)
Grainthorpe Primary School

It's So Early In The Morning

It's so early in the morning,
You can hear the sound of the day awakening,
The sound of spiders and beetles scuttling
Across the floorboards.

It's so early in the morning,
The ground is just beginning to frost,
The streetlights are still dimly lit in the mist.

It's so early in the morning,
You can only just see the sun's
Weak glow behind the trees,
Like a torch through a bush.

It's so quiet, you can hear a sparrow beat its wings,
And the sound of a twig snap, and an apple fall.

It's so early in the morning,
You see a fox paddling across the lane,
And a cat's tail swish through the air.

It's so early, you can hear a light switch click,
As a light flickers on.

It's so early in the morning,
You can see water creeping down a post,
Like cold down your spine,
It's so early in the morning.

Innes Adlard (11)
Grainthorpe Primary School

Yellow

Yellow is for daffodils,
Swaying in the wind.
Bees buzzing around their hives,
People growing sunflowers in their gardens,
Yellow for the beach,
On a hot summer's day,
When the sun is gleaming, shining away.

Daniel Rickett (9)
Grainthorpe Primary School

Blue

Blue is for the colour of my mum's car,
Blue is for the police cars rushing to the
Scene of the crime with their sirens flashing blue,
Blue is for the jumper I wear to school.
Blue is for the ocean, deep and dark,
Blue is for the bright blue sky with the white fluffy clouds,
Blue is for my writing book I write in every week,
Blue is the favourite colour of mine.

Jake French (11)
Grainthorpe Primary School

Yellow

Yellow is for daffodils,
Glowing in the sunlight.
Yellow is for yellow paint,
To brighten up your bedroom.
Children wearing yellow T-shirts,
Having great fun.
Yellow is for golden sun,
Yellow is for sandy beaches,
Waiting for people to come.

Lucia Willson (10)
Grainthorpe Primary School

The Dolphin

There once was a dolphin who lived in the sea,
He lived all his life all happy and free.
He swam and he splashed and did a big leap
Then he went down in the water ever so deep.
Beautiful fish swim in the sea,
That's all about the dolphin that lived in the sea.

Laura Vallely (6)
Kirkby-on-Bain CE School

The World As I Wish

I wish the world was a joyous land,
Where the beaches would have pink cooling sand.
The sky would be green and the grass would be blue,
The trees would be pale purple too,
They would have dragons and unicorns in the magical zoo,
The end of books would never come,
And they would have the most amazing food for your tum.
The dolphins there would swim and walk,
And all the animals would now talk.
We'd visit the most wondrous places,
And have sky-high flying races.
The houses would be gold with chocolate-running taps,
And there would be no need for such things as ridiculous maps,
There would be cute and cuddly *not* plague-spreading rats.
Everyone would stay up at night,
And a flying pig would not be an unusual sight.
There would be lollipop trees and sugar cube cars,
You could even go on holiday to Mars.
If only all this could be true,
We'd have the most fun ever, just me and you.

Nicola Hill (11)
Kirkby-on-Bain CE School

Mr Bounce

Mr Bounce was very small,
Like a rubber ball.
He just couldn't keep himself on the floor
And he bounced all over the place.
One day he bounced so high,
He went straight into outer space!

Edward Wright (9)
Kirkby-on-Bain CE School

The Three Rich Pigs

Once upon a rhyme
In the 1940s time
Lived three rich pigs
And they all wore wigs.
One purple, one blue and one red
But they had to go down the street, which they did dread.
They went in a limo, which was black
And when going in the shop they got attacked
Because they forgot their bodyguard,
Who they left in the yard.
They bought some sunglasses,
And some very strong mustard gases,
And then went home,
To the Millennium Dome.
At their house they went on the wheel,
Which was made out of steel.
They went to bed,
With a banging head.
After opening their Christmas hampers
Full of champers
They decided to visit the tower of Pisa,
Where they had to pay by Visa.
They climbed to the top,
Where all their jaws dropped
At the sight of the wolf, their old rival.
So they all screamed for survival,
Out of pure fear,
'I'm a celebripiggy get me out of here!'

Mia Falcidia (9)
Kirkby-on-Bain CE School

Favourites and Heroes!

Cadbury's are my hero,
For making my life worthwhile.
Without their chocs and other stuff,
I don't know what I'd do.

My friends are all so fab,
I see them all most days.
Each and every one of them
So cool in different ways.
They're definitely one thing I couldn't live without.

English is my favourite subject,
Writing stories, poems and lots, lots more.
But stories and poems
Beat them all as you kind of tell!

I consider candles
As very beautiful things.
They flicker and burn
With twists and turns
All the time with amazing colours.

So there you are
All my best and favourite things
Put in a poem
For lots of you to read!

Sophie Brass (11)
Kirkby-on-Bain CE School

Snow

S now falling from the sky
N ever knowing why
O n my hand
W inter's white wonderland.

Grace Lamyman (8)
Kirkby-on-Bain CE School

The Seasons

In spring *flowers* start to grow.
In summer *flowers* bloom.
In autumn the *leaves* fall of the trees.
In winter *everything* is bare.

Lucie Redwood (6)
Kirkby-on-Bain CE School

Ppppoem

My pet penguin Percy
Picked up a penicillin pill,
Put it in a proper parcel,
Plodded down the path,
Past the park,
To the post box
To post the parcel to his
Poorly pen pal Polly the *p-p-pretty* parrot.

Emma Lonsdale (9)
Kirkby-on-Bain CE School

Who Am I?

I am the sun, hot and yellow,
I am the wind, howling and strong,
I am the rain, wet and clear,
I am the snow, a blanket and cold,
I am the lightning, bright and striking,
I am the thunder, loud and scary.

So, what are *you*?

Amy Ball (10)
Kirkby-on-Bain CE School

The Dragon's Cave

In the dragon's cave there lay a green and speckled
Fire-breathing dragon.
Nobody dared to visit the cave
By reason of it being too intimidating.

She lay there all night, lonely
With nothing to do.
People thought she was a poor dragon
But no, there were more obnoxious things she could do.

At the very head of her cave
There was a sight saying
'Keep out, do not enter!'
So nobody ever did.

Everything was silent, nothing was moving
The fire-breathing dragon was fast asleep.
Nobody was there; maybe that's why nobody
Ever visited the dragon's cave.

Lauren Hunter (10)
Kirkby-on-Bain CE School

Skateboarding

Get your skateboard
Nice and clean
Now look! There's
A ramp to be seen.
Jump on your skateboard
Don't be scared -
Don't just stand there and have a stare.
Get some speed up, down the path
And try hard not to laugh.
Lean forward going up the ramp,
Do a backflip, then you'll be a champ.
Land down carefully, try not to fall
You may end up in a great, big ball.

Josh Hunter (8)
Kirkby-on-Bain CE School

Snow Is Beautiful

Snow is nice
Snow is cold
Snow is ice
Snow is white
Snow is light
Snow is crisp and bright.

Bernadette Hogg (8)
Kirkby-on-Bain CE School

The Full Moon

A lonely face,
A shining, shimmering ball.
When he drops his dust
The world turns to magic.
He is the ruler of the skies,
The god of the stars,
The holder of wishes,
A light when all light is gone.

Eleanor Redwood (10)
Kirkby-on-Bain CE School

Puddles

P laying in puddles, getting very wet,
U p to our middles in puddles.
D arting to and fro
D ozens of puddles everywhere you go.
L ying around, after the snow,
E veryone having fun until . . .
S unshine breaks through.

Hannah Brass (8)
Kirkby-on-Bain CE School

Space

Misty Mercury races
Through the night,

Venomous Venus
In dull and light,

Expensive Earth
Is sunny or grey,

Messy Mars
Is here to stay.

Jumping Jupiter
Jumps on the spot.

Silly Saturn
Summers are hot.

Unbelievable Uranus
Expected rain,

Nasty Neptune
Is really in pain.

Pluto is tiny and
Spins far away,

That's all the planets
There's no more to say.

Alice McConnon (9)
Kirkby-on-Bain CE School

Neil Armstrong

Neil Armstrong - far from home
Going into space.
The moon said, 'Neil Armstrong.
Will you come to me?'
Neil said, '1, 2, 3 and away!'

Rosie Harris (8)
Kirkby-on-Bain CE School

There's A Dragon In My House

There's a dragon in my house
He's tiny, his name is Nibbles.
As he eats, he grows,
He's as tall as me.
He ate my breakfast, the wallpaper
Not to mention my bed,
Now I sleep in a sleeping bag.
What will I do with him?
Should I look after him or
I could just abandon him?
No! I must look after him,
But he might eat my pets -
Nibbles might not like them.
On no, he's eating my bike!
No don't, please!

Callum Cheetham (8)
Kirkby-on-Bain CE School

Monopoly

Roll a dice
Think twice
Disappointment!

Pay fifty pounds
For one bit of ground
Go to jail!

Roll a double
Get out of trouble
You're a winner!

Tom Fox (9)
Monkshouse Primary School

If I Were A Champion

If I were a champion
I'd buy a mansion
With leather sofas
And four chauffeurs!
I'd have four Ferraris
And my garden would be a safari,
With a jacuzzi and a pool
I'd live in luxury, it would be so cool!
I'd have some butlers who'd serve me
I'd have some paintings for my visitors to see.
My garden would have a fountain
That goes as high as a mountain.
I would have a bar
In the shape of a car.

Jack Nottingham (9)
Monkshouse Primary School

My Mum

My mum has hair,
My mum has skin,
My mum can jump
My mum can run.
My mum can walk
But the thing I like is -
The love and cuddles.
That's what my mum can do
That's what my mum has in her heart . . .
Love!

Charles Chamberlain (10)
Monkshouse Primary School

The Rainbow Poem

Red are the roses
Swaying from side to side
Yellow is the sun
Beaming down on the Earth
Pink are the petals
Being watered
Green is the grass
On a warm day
Purple are the grapes
Glistening in the fruit bowl
Orange is the juice
Which we drink
Blue are the swings
That we play on.

Crystal Gray (9)
Monkshouse Primary School

Dragons

Blazing fire shining in the night,
Dragons' breath, killing flesh.
Fire-breathing monster that can kill
Almost anything,
Dragons are good for murdering.
They live in lava and can take the heat,
Dragons are racing in the sky.
A fire dragon's bloody teeth
Can cut through steel -
They make it into a tasty meal.

Gareth Ellis (10)
Monkshouse Primary School

My Brother

My brother is the best
Better than the rest.
He is so cool
My brother rules!

He's called Scott
I love him a lot
I wouldn't want anything but him.
He is the best
He is so cool
He rocks!

He never loses his glasses
They bend right back
He has a special teddy bear
He cuddles each night in bed.

His hobby is cooking
Just like me
He cooks, he sleeps
He sleeps, he cooks
He's my cute teddy bear.

Stacie Eden (11)
Monkshouse Primary School

Puppies

Puppies are cute, I love them
Puppies are fun
Come and join the game
I wish they were mine, all mine
Brown or black, I don't care
Because I love them anyway.
Puppies.

Josh Turner (10)
Monkshouse Primary School

If I Were A Footballer

If I were a footballer
I'd be seriously rich
All my fans would cheer me on
On the football pitch!

I would buy a mansion
With a jacuzzi and pool
Doing whatever I like
Wouldn't that be cool!

I'd sign lots of autographs
Each and every day.
I'd be the new David Beckham
But in my own way.
If I was a footballer
I'd be seriously rich
All my fans would cheer me on
The football pitch!

George Chandler (10)
Monkshouse Primary School

Dragons

The dragon's fiery breath burns my soul,
I think he's trying to say hello, hello!
I wish I could have a dragon as my pet,
Fly in the sky with him until the night gets wrecked.
Just look at the colourful scales he's got,
On his wings, his face, it's on the whole lot.
I bet this is just a dream of having one,
I wish I could feed him chocolate to fill his tum.
Now that morning's coming back -
I'd better stay with my rabbit, called Jack.

Cherie Payne (9)
Monkshouse Primary School

Rose Fairy

R oses smell so beautiful
O ur garden is full of them,
S o don't go in our garden, or you'll get a bite
E at up your plant food, or you won't be so beautiful.

F eed the plants, do not forget
A rose is like my mum.
I love roses, they're the best
R oses are red
Y ou are too!

Vicky Orme (10)
Monkshouse Primary School

My Family

You are the fizz in my cola
You are the petal on my flower
The bubbly chocolate in my Aero
Without you, I would be flat.

You are the fluffy bubbles in my bath
You are the apple of my eye
The heart in my body
Without you, I would drown.

Tegan Bates (9)
Monkshouse Primary School

My Mum

My mum is as fast as a cheetah when she's late
She's as funny as a hilarious clown
My mum is a big giant, looking over me
She's as kind as a really, posh servant
She's as scary as a mass murderer
And as protective as a leopard protecting her cubs
I love my mum!

Nathan John Spendelow (10)
Monkshouse Primary School

My Nanny

I'd like to tell you about my nan,
She's always losing things.
It was only just the other day,
She said, she'd lost her glasses.
When my nan found them she got in a flap,
It was twelve o'clock and she was late
For her cleaning job.
That's why I'd like to say my nan is the most
Forgetful elephant there is.

Lauren Morris (11)
Monkshouse Primary School

Good Memories

Kinder than any man I've ever seen
With his hat and boots
He would stroll down his garden
Without a care in the world

He loved racing pigeons
And growing his plants
He even did a dance
When he thought he'd won the lottery.
I love my grandad.

Matthew Smith (10)
Monkshouse Primary School

Dragon

D ragons are the best
R acing across the sky
A nimal eater
G one for years
O nly in books now
N obody cares about them anymore.

Oliver Smith (10)
Monkshouse Primary School

My Grandma

My grandma is cuddlier than the
Cuddliest teddy bear.
She is as warm as a red-hot radiator
And is a comedian always making me laugh
My grandma is an everlasting fire
She will never stop caring
And last of all, my grandma is always
There for me, through good times and bad.

Bethany Stinson (11)
Monkshouse Primary School

Having Fun

H appy having fun and games,
A n ice cream is very nice.
V arious flavours covered in ice
 I n my tummy goes the cream
N o more being on the football team
G o and play and have some fun

F un-filled action for everyone
U tterly butterly, tired out,
N o more fun till the next school's out!

Jake Worth (9)
Monkshouse Primary School

My Friend Rachel

Roses appearing in friendship
Apples we would eat together.
Cannot see her anymore,
Here and there I miss her
Even now I will cry
Little did I see her
But she was my best friend.

Aimee Lauren Chamley (10)
Monkshouse Primary School

My Teacher

My teacher is great
She really is our best mate.
Mrs Patman's classroom is cool,
It definitely is a great school.

Mr Gale is our headmaster
He can run much faster,
Mr Gale has a smart case
With a very funny face.

Jasmine Smith (10)
Monkshouse Primary School

My Daddy

My daddy is as soft as the cutest bunny,
He's as busy as a bee at work.
His laugh brightens up the room,
He's as funny as an hilarious comedian.
My daddy is a dolphin - kind to everyone
His laugh is as loud as thunder and lightning.

Kimberley Clasby (10)
Monkshouse Primary School

The Writer Of This Poem
(Based on 'The Writer Of This Poem' by Roger McGough)

The writer of this poem is . . .
A million people
As strong as a rock
As gentle as a cat.

As fast as a cheetah
As slow as a snail
As happy as a drunken man
As cool as sun glasses.

Jordan Fisher (9)
Monkshouse Primary School

The Writer Of This Poem
(Based on 'The Writer of This Poem' by Roger McGough)

The writer of this poem is . . .
As tall as a tree in the woods,
As strong as a hippo in Africa.
As gentle as a mouse in a hole,
As hungry as a tiger in a jungle.
As angry as a leopard in a race.
As noisy as a lot of monkeys
As sleepy as lots of polar bears on the ice.
As good as a frog jumping on a thin piece of rope.

Bethany Copland (9)
Monkshouse Primary School

Acrostic Poem

S now is cold
N o snow is warm
O ur snowmen are big
W e are building snowmen
M e and my brother had a snowball fight
E veryone is happy
N o one is sad.

Jake Haynes (10)
Monkshouse Primary School

Dragon

In the skies a dragon flies
He saw a man who was going to die,
He went to see if the man was alright and
The man told him he fell off a kite.
The dragon was so worried, he nearly cried
He called for help all day and night,
Eventually, someone came and made it alright.

Joseph Foster (10)
Monkshouse Primary School

I Know Someone

I know someone who can
ask questions for England.

I know someone who can smile
and there ears go up and down.

I know someone who can put a stone
on their elbow and scratch his elbow
from underneath it, then catch it
in one go.

I know someone who can do a front
and backflip on a bouncy castle.

I know someone who can
go cross-eyed.

I know someone who can beat
up their uncle.

I know someone who can make people
laugh when they're feeling down.

I know someone who can go up a tall
ramp on their BMX and get about
three feet off the floor.

And that someone is me!

Joshua Smith (10)
Monkshouse Primary School

My Rainbow Poem

Red are for roses on a summer's day
Orange is for a fire that crackles away
Yellow is a sun that shines on the ground
Green is for grass full of insects making a sound
Blue is for tears that run down my cheek
Indigo is the sea with seagulls that squawk
Violet is for the horizon that glimmers.

Georgia Lowe (9)
Monkshouse Primary School

Home Sweety Home

The fence is made out of lollipops
The roof is sugar candy,
If you get rather hungry
It could be quite handy.

The window ledge is chocolate
The grass is liquorice laces,
Through the sugar paper glass
You can see brown mice faces.

They're all sitting at a table,
Drinking cups of sherbert,
Who is in there?
It's Molly, Hugh and Herbert!

Eleanor Harrison (9)
Monkshouse Primary School

Snow

Snow on my house
Snow on a fieldmouse
Feel the winter glow
When it's about to snow
Freezing snow with a glow
Crunching, crispy, crunching
Feel the wind blow.

When it's freezing
I start wheezing
The snow is white
So I can see with all my might
Icy, crispy snow
Feel my blood flow.

Megan Thompson (8)
Morton CE Primary School

Night

Night is so horrifying, it scares you
        out of your skin.
Night makes you feel terrified in
        your depths of darkness.
Night gives you mystifying nightmares
        as it whirls up your spine.
Night is a burglar, stealing
        all your jewels
Laughing at you every night, making
        you feel ghouled
Night is like a mysterious creature
        with a long, black, eerie cloak.
An extremely bony skull and takes
        sharp steps, night is.

Sophie Stoyles (9)
Morton CE Primary School

A Winter's Day

On a winter's day
I got dressed to go to play
I saw something in the snow
And it glowed and it glowed.

It looked like some gold
But surely not that old.
It was very, very cold
And it was full of mould.

It's a very noisy place to be
Not for you, but it's for me.
A brilliant snowy day
Don't you agree?

Sebastian Murdoch (9)
Morton CE Primary School

Snow

Snow, snow on the ground,
I roll my snowball round and round,
Snow, snow, every where,
I roll my snowball without a care.

Snow is crunchy and crisp,
Snow falls by in a wisp
Freezing white ice
Run around, do little mice.

I like to sledge
When snow's upon the hedge.
Snow, snow, cold and slippery
I see a freezing hedgehog,
Oh so very prickly.

Snow is falling
When the day is dawning,
I love to build snowmen
Sometimes I see my friends
From Corby Glen.

Snow falls on the gate,
Inside, wait and wait.
My mum pours tea
Then I see the first spring bee.

Kayleigh Saunders (10)
Morton CE Primary School

Snow Is Falling

Snow, snow, very icy
and every day it seems to grow,
When I blow, it says 'Hello!'
And I say hello too.
When it falls, it falls slowly
Snow makes my toes cold,
Ice is slippery like soap.

Alice Green (9)
Morton CE Primary School

Snow Storm

The snow is cold
I have been told,
Beneath my knees
I shiver like the bees.

The wind is blowing, wilder and wilder,
In ten minutes' time, it gets milder and milder
Now it is ice,
And I'm feeling nice.

The butterflies are gone,
And everything has been done.
A blizzard is coming down to the town.

The snow is falling
And the day is dawning.
The sun is out
And I want to shout.

The clouds are breaking through,
I want to play with you.
The snow is coming again
The snow is building up on the pane.

Jessica Schaffer (8)
Morton CE Primary School

Snowstar

The snow falls down
Onto the ground,
I hear footsteps
Noises all around.

It is lonely,
The plain white of the snow.
The sun has gone
Feel the icy ground below.

Adam Smith (9)
Morton CE Primary School

Night

Kind, generous, caring, soft, gentle - that's what I am,
Comforting am I, don't worry, I'm as soft as a lamb.

Do I make you feel safe when I'm around?
Not giving you nightmares where you are drowned.

I am kind and caring like a loving aunt,
But give you sweets, I can't!

I'll make you welcome
I don't act dumb.

Soothing and sweet,
My face is beautiful to meet.

Twinkling, heavenly,
Sunrise eyes.
They're not part of a disguise.

A smiling mouth is mine,
My blonde flowing hair is fine.

White robes and golden dress,
I'm not an angel in distress.

Calming and welcoming, I move afar,
Warm and cosy, my thatched cottage door is ajar.

Take you to Heaven and give you sweet dreams, ta-ta!

Emma Marie Percy (10)
Morton CE Primary School

Snow

Snow that blows in the sky,
Snow that lands on the snowman.
I know that snow is on the go,
But on the top, the wind blows.
When the snow blows, it says, 'Hello!'
Snow's on the ground,
It's there! Never go snow!

Darren Storey (10)
Morton CE Primary School

Afternoon Poem

Afternoon ends
>with a dog barking.

Afternoon ends
>with a baby yelling.

Afternoon ends
>with a cat purring.

Afternoon ends
>with a kettle humming.

Afternoon ends
>with wheels squeaking.

Afternoon ends
>with leaves rustling.

Afternoon ends
>with me just listening

Afternoon ends
>happy afternoon.

Alice Howlett (7)
Morton CE Primary School

Snow Storm

The wind is blowing,
it keeps hailing and snowing,
outside is cold,
the lightning is bright gold.

I can see now, the ground is whiter
the sky is brighter,
the thunder and lightning has stopped
the snowing has dropped.

Now I can go out to play
and enjoy the rest of the day.

Tara Mason (9)
Morton CE Primary School

Afternoon Poem

Afternoon ends
    with a cat purring
Afternoon ends
    with babies yelling
Afternoon ends
    with my dad snoring
Afternoon ends
    with owls hooting
Afternoon ends
    with doors banging
Afternoon ends
    with roadwork's drilling
Afternoon ends
    with me sleeping because
    it's past my bedtime.

Rebecca Born (9)
Morton CE Primary School

Snow

Here comes snow,
as soft as dough.
When it blows
it'll freeze your toes.

It's slippery and white
and dazzles at night.
You can't fly a kite
but you can make anything bright.

Watch it glow
as you say, 'Hello!'
You can throw it,
you can catch it.
Here comes snow!

Abigail Howlett (9)
Morton CE Primary School

Night

I steal anything I can feel
In a house or up an ancient oak tree.

My rags are torn, rough and black
I am not seen when I kidnap.

From little kids I steal sweet dreams,
To see what things are in their heads.

I move like a panther, swiftly and smoothly,
My long, black cloak is covered with scales of a snake.

Quickly and quietly, I sneak in the shadows,
With my big black boots, stamping.

I steal anything I can feel
In a house or up an ancient oak tree.

Just watch out at night,
Because you'll be next.

Sweet dreams.

Bethany Fraser (10)
Morton CE Primary School

Snow Is Falling

I care about a bear,
who is very fair.
His name is Snowy bear.
He feels like snow
and his eye's glow,
like a glowing water flow.
Snowy bear is very slow,
because his tummy is so low.
Off we went with a ho, ho, ho.
I throw some snow
like I was in a show
Come on, we've got to go
before more snow.

Eden Andres (9)
Morton CE Primary School

Afternoon Poem

Afternoon ends
   With people chattering
Afternoon ends
   With scooters squeaking
Afternoon ends
   With bikes zooming
Afternoon ends
   With cars brumming
Afternoon ends
   With the wind blowing
Afternoon ends
   With workmen drilling
Afternoon ends
   With babies yelling
Afternoon ends
   With coats zipping
Afternoon ends
   With people chomping
Afternoon ends
   With doors banging.

Jack Sheppard (8)
Morton CE Primary School

Snow Time

Snow swirling
Snow twirling,
Snow whirling
Round and round.
Down and down
Watch the snow falling.

Children playing in the snow,
Toes and fingers, all aglow.
This is what they say all day
I wish it was like this every day.

Kieran Grafton (9)
Morton CE Primary School

Afternoon Poem

Afternoon ends
   with a cat purring
Afternoon ends
   with cars zooming
Afternoon ends
   with mummies mumbling
Afternoon ends
   with babies gurgling
Afternoon ends
   with the television chattering
Afternoon ends
   with owls hooting
Afternoon ends
   with me just listening
Afternoon ends
   and takes me to my bed
Afternoon ends
   and takes me to my bed.

Quiet and peaceful afternoon.

Ayisha Hanson (8)
Morton CE Primary School

Night

I met Night at midnight,
She stays in the dark shadows,
Her black plaited hair, streaked with red
Sways unseen.

Her cape swings in the darkness,
Wind howls around her feet.
Bad dreams contained in bottles,
Delivered through keyholes by straws of light.

Eleanor Farrow (10)
Morton CE Primary School

Night

Swaying through the wind, her leather jacket,
I met in the dark, the lonely night,
Inside the keyhole, there she's off.

Licking her black, evil lips, she spots the blood,
After tasting, she conceals her face.
Black hooded, she flies back to Hell.

Striding through the darkness like the wind,
The moths surround her red skull eyes,
Sparkling under the moon, her twilight feet.

Glowing red streaks through black dark hair,
Twinkling in the dark, her bright red crop top.
Leading the journey onwards, her sooty-black jeans.

Giving nightmares to you involves
Taking your spirit forwards to Hell.
Wicked dreams,
Goodnight!

Lauren Dilley (10)
Morton CE Primary School

Night

I am soft, kind and gentle
But never mental.

Glittering happily, my eyes are
Like the morning dew,
Swaying in the wind, my lilac robes
Remind me of you.

Into my world, I can welcome people,
The church which I pray in, has a steeple.

You can tell when I'm in a comforting mood,
Because I become as cool as you.

When I go, I will just gently drift away,
Like the breeze astray.

Gemma Dakin (9)
Morton CE Primary School

Afternoon Poem

Afternoon ends
   with a brown dog barking
Afternoon ends
   with men shouting
Afternoon ends
   with people laughing
Afternoon ends
   with boys snoring
Afternoon ends
   with footsteps squeaking
Afternoon ends
   with cars zooming
Afternoon ends
   with me, just listening
Afternoon ends -
   what a terrible afternoon!

Samuel Doe (7)
Morton CE Primary School

Night

My eyes are gleaming red
looking like they burn in the darkness.
My fluorescent green hair, glows
in the unlit day.
The face of night will never be seen.

My speed is as fast as a car,
then as slow as a slug.
But when I get tired I absorb into your shadow.

Whilst asleep, into your nightmare I will slip,
Then your family will be dead.

It makes me feel like I'm a devil,
Night will never be defeated,
now the sun has come, so I must go.

Jamie Cotter (11)
Morton CE Primary School

Medicine Man

Desert liver
Sickness killer
Potion maker
Love craver
Illness curer
Water pure
Animal carer
Evil snarer
Weather controller
Magic solver
Fruit picker
Metal miller
Living low,
Guess who?

Robert Mumby (10)
Morton CE Primary School

Afternoon Poem

Afternoon ends
    with an owl hooting
Afternoon ends
    with a man humming
Afternoon ends
    with a car crashing
Afternoon ends
    with the sea lapping
Afternoon ends
    with a girl bellowing
Afternoon ends
    with a bird cooing
Afternoon ends
    with me just listening
Afternoon ends -
    a hard, busy afternoon.

Daniel Jenkins (8)
Morton CE Primary School

Afternoon Poem

Afternoon ends
   with children laughing
Afternoon ends
   with a boy sneezing
Afternoon ends
   with coats zipping
Afternoon ends
   with my dog barking
Afternoon ends
   with owls hooting
Afternoon ends
   with the television chattering
Afternoon ends
   with me, just listening
Afternoon ends and takes me home from school
   it's been an exhausting afternoon.

Craig Turner (7)
Morton CE Primary School

Animal Poem

Monkey on he railway
Picking up nails
Along came an engine
And broke the monkey's tail.

Elephant on the railway
Sucking up junk
Along came an engine
And broke the elephant's trunk.

Snail on the railway
Looking at a bell
Along came an engine
And broke the snail's shell.

Tyler Burton (9)
New Leake Primary School

My Cat

My cat's fur is as soft as a feather,
She does not like the rainy weather.
She walks around, like she is clever
As long as I live, I will love her forever.

Megan White (9)
New Leake Primary School

The Pig Poem

Fat belly, full of food,
The pig grunted with happiness.
Trotting into the mud
Thick mud, squelching mud, smelly mud.

The big fat pig lay down,
Snorting cheerfully into the sty.

Funny little piglets,
Trot into their sty with joy,
Clumsy and cute, rolling in the mud.
Thick mud, squelching mud, smelly mud.

Their fat pink bodies, short curly tail
And muddy hooves
Rush toward their trough.
But we all know pigs go *'Oink!'*

Kayleigh Willoughby (10)
New Leake Primary School

School

S is for science, we do lots of tests
C is for colouring, I like that the best
H is for homework, we do it every night
O is for octagon, I hope I've drawn it right!
O is for outside, we play football in the yard
L is for learning, we have to try hard.

Rio Burton (10)
New Leake Primary School

Romeo And Juliet

I play the role of Juliet
Sitting on a garden bench,
Waiting for true love's kiss;
As we face eye to eye,
'I love you Juliet,' he will sigh.
And we blow a kiss for true love,
Calm and gentle; lip to lip!
And the audience softly sigh,
Some of them just sit and cry.
And I know deep inside
That when he looks at me;
The contact is eye to eye!
And how I wish he was mine forever.
But when the play is over,
I sigh to myself and sit on my bed,
Dreaming of that garden bench
And think to myself and call to him
As I whisper in his ear;

> 'That how could you be with me still
> Like dandelion and daffodil?
> And I don't want to forget the past
> So could our love be here to last?'

Lauren City (9)
St Gilbert's CE School, Stamford

Neptune

Neptune is the watery whale; it's always swimming
tear-filled.
But it is serving the planet Jupiter with its own
wine and wealth.
It is a danger for the sun it is the extinguisher of space.
It is cunning like a dolphin, sneaks there and
everywhere through the wide open space.

Charles Dickinson (9)
St Gilbert's CE School, Stamford

Last Minute Nerves

We lined up, row by row,
Ready to perform the Wizard of Oz show.
A pale faced girl leaves to be sick,
But really, it was a very sly trick.

The audience filed in through the door,
They sat crossed-legged on the wooden floor.
Sweat dripped from my face,
Two children started to talk,
The teacher was soon on their case.

Finally, the show began,
Starting with me, the Tin Man.
I, shaking because I had a main part,
Had to ask the Wizard for a heart.

Thankfully I remembered all my lines,
And luckily I did fine!
The whole show went well,
The teachers said that we excelled.

Hannah Cattell (11)
St Gilbert's CE School, Stamford

Midsummer Night's Dream

There 'twas, thy crack of dawn,
Near the forest with its meadowed lawn.
Romance is the fog that hangs in the air,
Hermia, Helena and Lysander.
Demetrius plotting by a babbling brook,
Disguised as a tree, was withering young Puck.
Titania and Oberon in the fairy realm,
Floating in a boat, fairies at the helm.
'I pray thee,' cried Titania, halting the boat.
'I am mortal, do not dote.'
Bottom was foolish, accepting her love,
She bought him a present, a white turtle dove.

Louisa Pini (11)
St Gilbert's CE School, Stamford

Appearing In A School Play

The day I appeared in a school play
Miss Mills said I was a Mary, on the way.
Jane and Jack said that it would be fine
but when I got on the stage, chills went down my spine.

The palms of my hands were sweaty and I felt like
the world was crashing in on me, and that was only
the rehearsals.
'It will be fine!' everyone said.

Hours turned into days, days into weeks
but still I was so nervous when I went to speak.
'Keep going!' said Miss Mills, 'You'll get
there in the end.' Practise, practise, practise
was the advice from my friends and so
like a trooper, I kept plodding on.
In time, the words came easy and
everything was fine.

So it just goes to show, good things come to
everyone who is willing to give things a go!

Sophie Earl (10)
St Gilbert's CE School, Stamford

Predator

The torrential rain is thorns
Digging into your skin.
Deadly poison, dripping from the crown
Of its spikes,
It belts fiercely at windows,
Spitting out splinters like an arrow
Shooting from its bow.

Annie Davis (10)
St Gilbert's CE School, Stamford

The Stranger

Sun shining brightly upon a dark body,
Lighting up his head and coat
Whilst clouds mist the sun
And reflections slowly glow.

In the dead sway of the trees
Sadly the gentle breeze rustles through
A stranger's hair
His eyes are closed.
He stands alone, looking up, watching
A damaged poster board fades away

As shadows of clouds disappear.
The evening sun sets,
Not even the stranger notices.

The moon rises and washes away the clouds
Slowly the stars begin to twinkle.
The stranger walks away from the bustling street,
Nothing is where the stranger once stood.

Now lies a coffin and flowers
People gather to say goodbye,
No more signs
No more people
Just grass and a stone engraved.
The dead sway of flowers.
In the now dusty street.

Samantha Skippon (11)
St Gilbert's CE School, Stamford

I Am The Mind

I am the mind that enters the thought,
I am the lesson that's taught the pupil.
I am the page that turns the hand,
I am the story that starts the spark,
I am the sum that adds the scholar.
I am the race that runs the child,
I am something new that teaches the student.

Christina E Campbell (10)
St Gilbert's CE School, Stamford

In The Pet Shop

In the pet shop there was a . . .
woof, growl, chitter-chatter
miaow and co-loo-doo!

Dogs hear
Cats eating lots of fish
Rabbits half asleep
Fish all over you.

In the pet shop there was a . . .
woof, growl, chitter-chatter
miaow and co-loo-doo!

Fish making glub-glub-glub sounds,
Rabbits, fluffy as a dog.
Fish swimming around the tank,
Dogs in a kennel.

In the pet shop there was a . . .
woof, growl, chitter-chatter
miaow and co-loo-doo.

Zantia Pinner (8)
St Helena's CE Primary School, Willoughby

In The Jungle

*In the jungle, tigers fled
Some animals are falling dead.*

Tamers making leopards eat
Monkeys smoking in the heat
Tigers eating lots of meat
Gorillas gossip, like in a street.

*In the jungle, tigers fled
Some animals are falling dead.*

Tigers ignoring
Lions roaring
Monkeys barmy
The men in the army.

*In the jungle, tigers fled
Some animals are falling dead.*

Jack Whitmore-Finney (7)
St Helena's CE Primary School, Willoughby

At The Zoo

*Snap, growl, hiss, splish, splash, splish, splash
Hear the monkey's bananas go crish, crash, crish, crash*

Seals whining at your feet
Just for something to eat
Lots of folk, coming to see
That naughty, cheeky monkey.

*Snap, growl, hiss, splish, splash, splish, splash
Hear the monkey's bananas go crish, crash, crish, crash*

Silvery snakes go ssss
Monkeys echo
You naughty slippery, slimy gecko.

*Snap, growl, hiss, splish, splash, splish, splash
Hear the monkey's bananas go crish, crash, crish, crash.*

Harriet Hanwell (7)
St Helena's CE Primary School, Willoughby

Grandparents

Grandmas are everywhere, they may be wrinkled
and old, but I don't care!
My grandma used to go to dog showings,
nearly always came first or second.

Grandparents!
Grandads are everywhere, they may be wrinkled
and old, but I don't care!
My grandad is good at mowing the lawn and fixing things.

Grandparents!
Grandparents are wonderful but when you put them together
it is double to me!

Grandparents!

Amanda Dennis (8)
St Helena's CE Primary School, Willoughby

Pet Shop

Pet shop loud screams
Pet man proud, beams

Dogs sleeping
Cats peeping
Birds flying
people buying

Pet shop loud screams
Pet man proud, beams

Smells pony
Birds flow
Is long
Cows moo

Pet shop loud screams
Pet man proud, beams.

Rebecca Murray (9)
St Helena's CE Primary School, Willoughby

Trees

*In the tree hear the birds
Spitting out with tweeting words.*

Birds eating
Nuts and seeds
Squirrels, trees
Birds sleeping

*In the tree hear the birds
Spitting out with tweeting words.*

Fighting squirrels in the tree
While the birds collect worms
Sparrows fight to a treetrunk
Bluebirds flutter their wings

*In the tree hear the birds
Spitting out with tweeting words.*

Alexandra Cairns (8)
St Helena's CE Primary School, Willoughby

Cats

Cats are the best when they lay on their mats
Because they are very different to rats
They run around in the garden and think,
Where is my food today?
While the adults are busy in the kitchen
Preparing food for that day
Cats get in a mardy mood when they can't go to sleep
The children take no notice and start to shout,
Bleep! Bleep! Bleep!

Carly Hodson (10)
St Helena's CE Primary School, Willoughby

The Swamp

Hiss, croak, hiss
Please don't miss

Alligators swimming
Flies are irritating
Monkeys have to limp
Monkeys climbing trees

Hiss, croak, hiss
Please don't miss

Birds give a *splish, splash, splosh*
Crocs live on squeaky rats
Monkeys have to get some nosh
Crocs think monkeys are fat

Hiss, croak, hiss
Please don't miss

The water tastes brill for crocs
But not for pupils wearing frocks
Crocks love the taste of snakes
But crocs don't love the taste of stakes

Hiss, croak, hiss
Please don't miss.

Christopher Hill (8)
St Helena's CE Primary School, Willoughby

Jesus

J esus died when he was 33, they say
E nd of Jesus, but he came back alive
S ome of his friends were sad
U nder a large rock and left him there to die
S ome of his family were sad as well.

Charlotte Ranshaw (7)
St Helena's CE Primary School, Willoughby

Acrostic Poem

C andles glowing
H olly tingling
R udolph flying the town
I love Christmas
S anta delivers presents
T rees have decorations on
M y! What a frosty day
A ngels flying
S anta is great!

Jessica Bainbridge (7)
St Helena's CE Primary School, Willoughby

My Dog Blackie

My dog has a furry tail
He always wakes me up
He jumps up onto our bed
Every morning

At breakfast when we feed him
He always wolfs it down
He never stops when eating
Every time

We take him for a walk
Morning, noon and night
He sometimes goes very fast
Every day

He sleeps on a fluffy cushion
In his basket on the floor
He creeps into my bedroom
Every night.

Peter Weatherley (8)
St Hugh's School, Woodhall Spa

Boredom Is

Boredom is when your dad turns on the news
Boredom is working all day,
Boredom is lying in bed until you go to sleep
Boredom is tidying up
Boredom is waiting till it's your turn
Boredom is tucking your shirt in,
Boredom is waiting to go up in dorms,
Boredom is getting into trouble
Boredom is looking for words in the dictionary
Boredom is when you go clothes shopping
Boredom is going to a CD shop
Boredom is boring
Boredom is zzz zzz zzz.

Alicia Emma Stevens (8)
St Hugh's School, Woodhall Spa

About My Dog Alby

He's white, he's white,
His name is Alby,
I love him, I love him, I love him so much,
He's cute, he's cute, he lives at Abbey Close.

He does tricks, he does tricks, he does backflips off the sofa,
He's crazy, he's crazy, he goes nuts,
He's my boy, he's my boy, I love him so much.

He's sweet, he's sweet, he is so lovely,
He's white, he's white and so fluffy,
He's quiet, he's quiet,
He's lonely, he's lonely, he's lonely when I'm gone.

Kieran Godwin (9)
St Hugh's School, Woodhall Spa

My Happiness

My happiness is blue as the clouds in the sky
It tastes like ripe pears in a pear tree,
It smells like sweet roses
It looks like a beautiful white rabbit
It looks like fluffy white clouds ready to
Pour down rain
It feels like soft tiger skin on my bed.

Caroline Elkington (7)
St Hugh's School, Woodhall Spa

Boredom Is . . .

Boredom is lying awake.
Boredom is waiting in a queue.
Boredom is watching people kissing.
Boredom is watching 'I'm A Celebrity, Get Me Out Of Here!'
Boredom means being bored.
Boredom is listening to the teacher.
Boredom is writing a story.
Boredom is boring.

Jordan Cox (8)
St Hugh's School, Woodhall Spa

My Shyness

My shyness is as grey as the autumn mist,
It tastes like peaches being picked,
It smells like a cake baking,
It looks like a bird,
Sounds like leaves falling.
It's cold, crumbly and makes me dance.

Evie Kimsey (8)
St Hugh's School, Woodhall Spa

Mother Nature

Mother Nature is the creation of life.
She blows her breath through the trees.
She controls the anger of the seas.
She grows the redwood from a seed.
She helps the antelope start off its life.
Mother Nature tries to get grass to grow.
But we destroy it to let oil flow.
She gives water for fish to thrive,
But we take that water so that fish cannot survive.
She brings up the elephant mighty, big and strong,
But we come and kill it for its ivory.
So please don't harm Mother Nature,
For she is doing you good.
She rears you from a baby,
She's trying to do you good.
So next time there's a nettle, do not whack it down,
Just think of Mother Nature and leave it standing tall.

Davyd Greenish (11)
St Hugh's School, Woodhall Spa

Home Life Nonsense Poem

I can smell the Lego cooking in the oven,
I can touch the boiling water hidden in the freezer.
I can hear the grapes chattering away in the sandpit.
I can see the mint shampooing its hair,
I can taste the fire swimming in the sink.

I can smell the cupboards sleeping in the fire,
I can touch the sound of the telephone ringing.
I can hear the carpet swaying in the breeze,
I can see the air playing cards,
I can taste the toaster burping!

Jacob Lawson (8)
St Hugh's School, Woodhall Spa

The Shoe

It has a tongue that cannot taste
It has a sole that cannot die.
It has eyes that cannot see
Some of them are made out of leather
Or other materials.
Everybody has them . . .
What am I?

Sarah Padley (8)
St Hugh's School, Woodhall Spa

Sadness

My sadness is like the yellow of the sun
It tastes like a salty chip, in the cold air
Smells like the salt of the sea
Looks like hailstones falling
Sounds like snow crunching
Feels like earthquakes.

Aimee Fry (7)
St Hugh's School, Woodhall Spa

Happiness

My happiness is red, the colour of jam
My happiness tastes of doughnuts the colour of brown
My happiness smells of chocolate dark brown
My happiness is round and fat like doughnuts
My happiness sounds like splashing in puddles
My happiness is warm water.

James Riggall (7)
St Hugh's School, Woodhall Spa

Gold

Gold is shiny
Gold is yellow
Gold is fun
Gold is bright
Gold is *big*
Gold is perfect.

Olivia Shelbourn (8)
St Hugh's School, Woodhall Spa

Horse

It lives in a field,
It's big and brown,
It's got a mane and
It can be big or small.
It goes clip-clop,
It's a horse!

Constance Read (7)
St Hugh's School, Woodhall Spa

My Happiness

My happiness is red like a cherry cake
It tastes like a smooth cherry
My happiness is like chocolate
It feels like splashing in puddles
After it has rained
A smooth chocolate.

Charlie Lundgren (8)
St Hugh's School, Woodhall Spa

My Happiness Is . . .

My happiness is light blue and it feels like the sea on the beach
It tastes like sandwiches
It smells like fresh flowers under the trees
It looks like a sunset going down beneath the trees
It sounds like jingling bells and it feels like soft teddies.

Zoe Furness (7)
St Hugh's School, Woodhall Spa

Christmas Day

I love Christmas,
We decorated the classroom.
I love Christmas.
We can have Christmas presents
I love Christmas
We had a late night
I love
Christmas Day.

Carrie Chan (10)
St Hugh's School, Woodhall Spa

Proud Is . . .

Proud is white
And tastes like lemonade,
It smells of sweet cherries.
It looks like a smart me!
It sounds like a clock ticking on the fireplace.
It feels like sitting in a comfy chair
Talking to your friend,
I feel like a king.

Dan Elkington (7)
St Hugh's School, Woodhall Spa

He's My Dog Max

His nose is wet
His eyes are brown
His fur is like a bear
He's my little dog Max
He runs like a cheetah
He lives in my house
He's my little dog Max
He likes going for walks
He's orange and black
He's my little dog Max.

James P Rollinson (9)
St Hugh's School, Woodhall Spa

My Vampire

My vampire - he has no name
He sucks the blood of anyone
He loves his meat
He loves the dog
He will always
Be my vampire dog.

Victoria Elkington (10)
St Hugh's School, Woodhall Spa

War In Normandy

We were sitting in our trenches
The bullets were flying over our heads
The man next to me was dead.
'Charge!' We ran from the trenches,
Mortars were going off!
Bang! Bang!
I fired
We took some prisoners.

Matthew Lyon (10)
St Hugh's School, Woodhall Spa

My Dogs

My dogs are funny things in the snow.
They love it!
Bounce, bounce.
I love my dogs and they love me.
They feel so furry.
Wag, wag! They wag their tails.
Bark, bark at the door,
Knock, knock - that's the door.
Bark! Bark!

Peter Duncanson (10)
St Hugh's School, Woodhall Spa

Fish

Fish are silent as they move,
Going through the freezing water,
A tiny trickle is made,
Jaws as powerful as frogs' legs,
With a scaly body and smelly breath,
And sharp teeth to bite its prey.

Alex Bake (10)
St Hugh's School, Woodhall Spa

Wind

Wind rustles through the trees,
and whistles a sea breeze.
It scares you on dark nights,
and gives such a fright.
It takes deep breaths,
you'd think brings death.
And takes long strides,
that sometimes collide.
It is like a ghost.

Phoebe Haller (10)
St Hugh's School, Woodhall Spa

The Outside World In Winter

In the deep mid-winter, the outside world is used with despair,
for no one's there, not even a sparrow, all inside keeping warm
by the fire.
Meanwhile outside, the grass as crisp as toast, tipped off
with the mist, making it as white and as damp as snow,
while the sun shines delicately through the mist, making
a glance through the trees, while their shadows dismiss.
The grass is lovely, no footprints in sight, for the outside world
is as lovely as at night.
Not a sound, not even a whisper, even two hours later,
no trail, no whisper.
'For it is not fair,' the trees say, 'how come it's Summer
that gets all the play?'

Sarah Richards (10)
St Hugh's School, Woodhall Spa

Pollution

Pollution is really very bad
It makes the plants look rather sad
It flows in the streams
It lingers in the air
It kills most animals
Along with the hare
It can cause damage
On Earth in a way
Earth may not come back
Even if we pay
So please protect the Earth
And you shall thank it one day.

Matthew Tilley (10)
St Hugh's School, Woodhall Spa

Boys And Bedrooms

There's a boy in my bedroom Mum,
He's attacking me like mad,
He'll never ever stop Mum,
I'll never get out.

He's gone under the bed now,
And I'm on the top,
He's acting like a monkey,
Swinging in the trees.

Now he's jumping on top of the bookshelf,
What am I going to do?
He will really never stop Mum,
He's giving me a fright.

There's a boy in my bedroom Mum;
He's attacking me like mad,
He'll never ever stop Mum,
Get my brother *out!*

Harriet Stovin (9)
St Hugh's School, Woodhall Spa

Tiger In The Garden

Here lies a tiger in our back garden,
A funny kind of tiger, not fat, not thin,
Neither tall nor short, for all he does is lie there.
His body is orange and black striped from head to toe,
He breathes heavily as he sleeps.
I wonder what tigers eat . . . ?
Meat I suppose, I could give him Tango our dog,
Probably I shouldn't.
Wow, I think he is waking up.
I should get a picture now that it is eating Mum's flowers . . .
Oh, it's gone.

Thomas Shelbourn (10)
St Hugh's School, Woodhall Spa

Chocolate Nonsense!

Chocolate, chocolate everywhere,
It always appears now and there.
But I wish it was always here,
Hopefully very near!

Chocolate's yummy,
Chocolate's scrummy,
How I love it,
Yum-yum!

Chocolate, chocolate smooth and creamy,
Oh it makes me so, so dreamy.
How I hope it never dies,
And I hope it never tries.

Chocolate's yummy,
Chocolate's scrummy,
How I love it,
Yum-yum!

Chocolate, chocolate light and fair,
All wrappers contain that I declare.
Sinking your teeth into that delight,
Is always a good way to start the night.

Chocolate's yummy,
Chocolate's scrummy,
How I love it,
Yum-yum!

Peter Watson (8)
St Hugh's School, Woodhall Spa

My Dog

Betty
Happy, playful, good
As furry as a squirrel
Never forgotten.

Tobias Downes (8)
St Hugh's School, Woodhall Spa

Chocolate, Chocolate

Chocolate, chocolate
Whirly and smooth
It appears here
And it appears there
It appears nearly everywhere

Unwrapping chocolate
Just feels great
But eating it is just like being on another planet

Chocolate, chocolate
Tasty and smooth
It appears here
And it appears there
It appears nearly everywhere.

    Chocolate, chocolate
    Just feels great!

Hannah Done (8)
St Hugh's School, Woodhall Spa

Lonely Monkey

I'm stuck behind these bars,
I don't know what to do,
I don't know how to get out of here,
What shall I do?

People watching over me,
Knocking on my bars,
I'm trying to get some sleep here,
But I can hear the cars.

I'm trapped here in this zoo,
Nothing really much to do,
Sleeping, eating all day long,
Oh I wish Mum was here too!

Daisie Winwright (10)
St Hugh's School, Woodhall Spa

Chickens

Chickens here
Chickens there
Chickens scattered everywhere!

Chickens in the garden
Chickens up the tree
I tell them they can peck at grass
But don't peck me!

Chickens here
Chickens there
Chickens scattered everywhere!

Cockerels crowing loudly
Pullets laying eggs
And they wake up in the morning
They exercise their compact legs.

Chickens here
Chickens there
Chickens scattered everywhere!

William Fowkes (9)
St Hugh's School, Woodhall Spa

The Tennis Ball

Bang! The ball flew over the net at terrifying speed.
Speeding towards the ground like a plane shot out of the sky.
Bounce!
Then silence, like nothing exists but you're like those
Unsuspecting dinosaurs who get blown up by a crater.
Then *thwack!*
That's the crater crashing to Earth
And you're off again.
Flying through time and space.
Then over the net, you know another crater is going to explode,
You just don't know when!

Alex Lawson (10)
St Hugh's School, Woodhall Spa

Limericks

There once was a teacher, Ms White,
Who one day had a very big fright,
She saw a big mouse,
Right inside the house,
She sat in a chair all up tight.

There was a man, Mr White,
Who had a peculiar kite,
It was yellow and red,
He flew it in bed,
His mates named him Peculiar White.

Nathan Kimsey (10)
St Hugh's School, Woodhall Spa

The Cake

The cake is for my tea,
Well, I hope it's for me,
It looks gooey and chewy and rich and nice,
I hope it doesn't get eaten by mice.

It's absolutely enormous,
As big as a brontosaurus (almost!)
The decorations on top are 10 feet tall,
With icing, chocolate, sprinkles and silver balls.

The flavour is chocolate, one of the best,
I hope it isn't eaten by all of the rest.
Mum shouts to me, 'It's time for tea!'
Yum! Yum! Chocolate cake for me, yippee!

Felicity Greenish (11)
St Hugh's School, Woodhall Spa

Try Your Best

Have a go you never know!
You'll sing this song all day
If you try to do things
You'll laugh and sing and play.

Have a lovely day today
The neighbour would reply
You're guaranteed to shine all day
And this is the reason why!

Have a go you never know!
You'll sing this song all day
If you try and do things
You'll dance and sing and play.

Amy Furness (9)
St Hugh's School, Woodhall Spa

Monsters

Monsters, monsters everywhere,
on the roof and in my hair
Monsters, monsters moan and groan,
in the bath and on the phone.
Monsters, monsters play and dance,
in the hall and at my house.
Monsters, monsters blink and wink,
in my sink and that is pink.
Monsters, monsters everywhere,
have a laugh and then stare . . . *go away!*

Emily O'Hara (10)
St Hugh's School, Woodhall Spa

Puddings

It's as sticky as super glue,
And as sweet as plums,
As sour as lemons and sherbet,
It smells as nice as flowers,
As hot as volcanoes,
As melted as a hot day,
As chocolately as Cadbury's World,
As sloppy as slugs,
As slithery as a bunch of snakes,
As dull as the colour black.

Antonia Caranza (11)
St Hugh's School, Woodhall Spa

Chocolate!

Chocolate, chocolate, I eat it everyday!
Munch, munch! Crunch, crunch!
During work, rest and play.
Mars, Bounty, Milky Way, all those bars,
Ready for another day.

Tamara Walker (9)
St Hugh's School, Woodhall Spa

My Dad

My dad is gross because he burps after lunch,
He burps after tea,
And you don't want to know what he does at breakfast,
But when we go on holiday he pushes me in the sea,
He pushes me in the pool,
But we always have fun,
But when Mum hears me and Dad fight,
She gets up tight and she smashes the light,
Preventing a fight!

Andrew Avison (10)
St Hugh's School, Woodhall Spa

My New Car

My new car is very shiny red,
It has lots of gadgets,
It is very speedy and strong,
It has leather seats and it has a CD player,
Its name is a Ferrari Enzo and it is very fast.

Matthew Stovin (10)
St Hugh's School, Woodhall Spa

Toffee

It's chewy,
It's sweet,
It's sticky,
It's gooey,
It's stuck in my hair,
It's lovely,
It's amazing,
It's fantastic,
It's wonderful,
Just eat it before it goes out of date,
Yuck!

Esther Malcolm (9)
St Hugh's School, Woodhall Spa

Shetland

A Shetland is as fat as a sausage
A Shetland is as shaggy as a sheepdog
A Shetland is as cheeky as a monkey
A Shetland's mane is as fluffy as a feather boa
A Shetland's tail is as spikey as a pineapple.
I love Shetlands!

Mathilda Dennis (10)
St Hugh's School, Woodhall Spa

Jelly

Jelly, it wobbles on my plate,
Wibble, wobble, wibble, wobble,
Strawberry, raspberry, lemon too,
Which one's for you?
Jelly wobbles in my mouth,
Munch, munch, wobble, wobble,
Lemon makes your lips go sour,
Raspberry makes your mouth full of power.

Gemma Kimsey (9)
St Hugh's School, Woodhall Spa

Max My Dog

Max perished ages ago,
We were full of sorrow.
When he died,
We cried.
We were all full of misery,
When he died.
He must have cried,
Because he was without his family.
He will always be
In Heaven.

Natalie Wilderspin (9)
St Hugh's School, Woodhall Spa

The Scary Monster

The monster has big eyes,
When you see it, it will give you a surprise.
The monster has big teeth,
He will eat you like a piece of beef.
The monster has a big body shaped like a dragon,
When you see it, it will be riding on a wagon.

Tom Craven (9)
St Hugh's School, Woodhall Spa

My New House

I've just been accommodated from college,
I'm at my new house,
It's rather small and cramped.
The cooker isn't working,
The electricity isn't on,
There are cockroaches on the floor,
Now I know why the house was only £50.

Huw Greenish (9)
St Hugh's School, Woodhall Spa

Monster

There's a monster in my bedroom Mum,
I'll tell you what it's like,
Its head is like a pumpkin,
Its claws are like a dragon,
Its body is like a worm,
Its teeth are like a shark,
I know you don't believe me Mum,
But hurry up, it's getting closer,
It's . . . aaarrrggghhh!

Arthur Brown (9)
St Hugh's School, Woodhall Spa

The Monster

There's a monster in the bathroom,
I'll tell you what it is like,
Its body is like a snake,
It went down the drain.
Its breath is like the desert,
And its teeth are yellow.
It's lucky I never saw
That monster ever again.

Daniel Hallett (9)
St Hugh's School, Woodhall Spa

My Pussy Cat

I love my pussy cat
her name is Tabbitha
she's a striped cat
Tabbitha rolls
and plays and sleeps
and hunts in the night
in the morning
when I wake up
Tabbitha is talking to me
now I look out of my window
but she's not there
I don't ever see her
she has disappeared.

Alana Howe (9)
St Hugh's School, Woodhall Spa

My Dog

Lucy
Fluffy, playful and she pounces around in the garden
And as loveable and she loves us like a lovebird
And up, up, up, up and away
She goes up there
Alone.

Heather Marsay (8)
St Hugh's School, Woodhall Spa

Love

Grandpa, Grandpa,
Come back now,
I love you,
I love you,
Please, please,
Come back now.
My mum loves you,
My dad loves you,
We all love you,
Come back,
Come back,
Please.

Charlotte Hanes (8)
St Hugh's School, Woodhall Spa

My Little Kittens

My little kittens, my little kittens
They pounce all day and pounce all night
My little kittens, my little kittens
They purr all day and dream all night
My little kittens are soft and sweet
They jump up and down like baby kangaroos
When my little kittens pounce to their bed
They curl into fluffy balls
Then snuggle each other.

Jacqui Baxter (9)
St Hugh's School, Woodhall Spa

A Summer Song

This is how the summer starts,
With flowers, leaves and the sun,
And all things bright and beautiful,
The season has begun.

Flowers open elegantly,
Gleaming with bright colours,
Leaves are turning luscious green,
Calves huddle to their mothers.

Fields are filled with ripened crops,
As harvesting is near,
Farmers and machines are getting ready,
As rabbits stop to hear.

Owls awaken with alert,
To start their hard night's work,
Down in the forest, deep below,
The victims begin to lurk.

So all of this is happening,
And four long months have passed,
With all the seasons yet to come,
The summer has gone fast!

Chloe Slater (10)
Stickney CE Primary School

Was I There?

Was I there? Was I there?
Floating by the sea.
Was I there? Was I there?
Where could I have been?

Was I there? Was I there?
Watching down on you.
Was I there? Was I there?
When you were so new.

Was I there? Was I there?
Flying in the sky.
Was I there? Was I there?
Flying very high.

Was I there? Was I there?
Breathing in the air.
Was I there? Was I there?
When I should have cared.

I wasn't there! I wasn't there!
Being there for you.
I wasn't there! I wasn't there!
To help see your life through.

Athena Pears (10)
Stickney CE Primary School

Snow White And The Seven Doors

Once upon a time,
People listened to my rhyme.
She was called Snow White,
Who got captured one dark night.

The castle is classified,
The captor is not identified.
Mrs White tries to escape,
Then found her magic cape.

Next she finds seven doors,
And seven floors.
And opened the sixth door found,
And fell through the ground.

She lit a match,
And in a dark patch,
Found Carlsberg express,
With a nice dress.

In another corner she found a torch,
Which lit up the massive porch,
With a backpack of beer,
She knew the end was near.

At last she made her escape,
Using her magic cape.
It had now fallen dark,
So she crept away from the airy park.

Once upon a time,
People listened to my rhyme.
She was called Snow White,
Who got captured one dark night.

Jamie Pewton (11)
Stickney CE Primary School

The Haunted House Of Time

Here is a tale you will never forget,
Lock up your doors and hold your pets.
The hour has come to tell my rhyme,
About 'The Haunted House of Time'.

Inside the haunted house of time,
Lives a man that isn't kind,
If strangers come, they do not go,
He asks them questions they do not know.

He wears a long and straight black cape,
To cover up his withered shape,
With fangs for teeth and two red eyes,
Start to worry! It is not a disguise.

The haunted house he has made his home,
In there he hides, all alone.
Hidden in corners and under stairs,
He gives unwary, awful glares.

During the day there is no sight or sound,
It's at night he moves around,
From room to room by candle light,
It really is an eerie sight.

Now you've heard this tale of mine,
About the haunted house of time,
I hope you consider the thought,
Of being snatched or even caught,
By the man who lives forever,
In the haunted house of terror!

This tale of mine,
'The Haunted House of Time',
Seems strange to some, to others gory,
But to me it's a tale or even a story.

Pamela Leigh (10)
Stickney CE Primary School

Homework

I know I did my homework Sir,
Of course I handed it in.
I could never lose it Sir,
Because I always win.

Do you think my pet would eat it?
I know aliens are not true!
My parrot would never eat it Sir,
And I wouldn't flush it down the loo.

I know I bought it in today,
My mates would never steal.
So let me off, what do you say?
If I have to, I will beg and kneel.

I know you think I'm joking Sir,
But really I am not.
I'm telling you it was here,
Oh! Why don't you believe me Sir?
I'm getting very hot!

Thomas Scott (10)
Stickney CE Primary School

Totally Devoted

There was a young man from Peckham
Who simply adored David Beckham
He moved down to Spain
And watched every game
He even found Fergie to deck him.

James Naylor (11)
Stickney CE Primary School

War

The war has started people feeling parted,
They feel alone and so cold-hearted,
Soldiers come from miles, miles afar,
Boarding vehicles, more complex than a fast Jaguar!

Now they're setting off for war,
Getting prepared for blood and gore,
They're at the intense, really awful battle scene,
Loading guns, all the soldiers seem keen.

Mounding some guns, hand in hand,
They're shooting at the very high guarded land,
Sergeants moving up the high, marshy hill,
Shouting, yelling, some keep still!

In the really fiery, acidy, high explosive sky,
Running fast, leaping high,
They're almost there,
Shooting at the planes so rare.

They've done it, they've won this dangerous war!
Checking all dead soldiers all is gore.
Running to the armoured killing machines,
Driving out of cold, lonely battle scenes.

They now are home with their loves,
They see the tears in their eyes,
Loved with surprise, cheering no more war,
England no longer sees blood and gore.

Andrew Houldershaw (10)
Stickney CE Primary School

The Wanderer

No one knows where she came from,
No one knows where she's going.
She haunts the towns at the dead of night,
Her pace never slowing.

There is no light in her eyes,
Her heart is as cold as stone,
She has no friends and no family,
She has no bed nor home.

Towards the blue sea she's drawn,
Although nobody knows why,
Some say she is cursed or is a ghost,
Some say they've heard her cry.

Some say she comes from afar,
Where giants and dragons hide,
Many say she is just an orphan,
Whose parents long ago died.

But she is a wanderer,
Whose deep down sadness does grow,
For everyone stares, and jeers at her,
Why's that? Nobody knows.

The salted wind whipped her hair,
She faced the thrashing blue sea,
She sat upon a moss covered rock,
And wished there silently.

A huge storm began to blow,
And she slowly turned to stone,
For evermore she looked out to sea,
And finally, she was home.

Heather Guy (11)
Stickney CE Primary School

The Death Of A Big Mac

Employees all of every sort,
Give ear unto my rhyme.
And if you find it wondrous short,
It will not make you whine.

Now listen to my tale of sadness,
It's sure to make you cry.
I'm just a Big Mac, it's sheer madness,
Why do I even try?

I sit next to my buddy, Fries,
Wet and covered in sauce.
I wonder, *can they hear my cries?*
But am I the main course?

This guy called Bill, he picks me up,
As horror strikes my face.
While Fanta's poured into a cup,
This is a real disgrace!

I'm taken out of my foamy box,
He opens his mouth wide.
He has sharp teeth like a vicious fox,
I thought I'd surely died.

But no, I'm travelling down his gut,
I'm in the stomach bay.
It's cold, damp and dark, but
I think I've had my day!

(No Big Macs were harmed during the making of this poem!)

Nicholas Appleyard (11)
Stickney CE Primary School

Pirates Of The Caribbean!

Many films have come and gone,
But this film is definitely number one,
The Black Pearl is a scary ghost ship,
Each of the sails has a great big rip.

My favourite character is Elizabeth Swan,
It just wouldn't be the same if she was gone,
Pirates of the Caribbean is the best film I've seen,
Just watching it makes you want to scream.

The pirates are scary but funny too,
But most of the time they jump out on you,
Will Turner is brave and he can fight,
He cares about Elizabeth day and night.

The pirates are looking for the necklace of gold,
It involves some sort of curse that's what everyone's been told,
Another of my favourites is Jack Sparrow,
He is a pirate from tip to toe.

Ships fight and bombs hurl,
The wars are between the Interceptor and the Black Pearl,
Fighting people is Jack Sparrow's thing,
And he acts like he's the king,
So in the end all the pirates die,
And that's where they'll always lie.

Emilie Kerr (10)
Stickney CE Primary School

The 14th Floor

I was once in an elevator like I was up in the air.
When all of a sudden something gave me a scare!
It was the elevator and I was all on my own,
When I pulled out of my pocket a mobile phone!

The elevator had stopped, it was such a shock!
And all I could hear was my dog, and watch, tick-tock.
I was scared but jolly,
As I had my shopping and border collie.

But what was I thinking, I could ring the shop.
So I rang the shop and told them I was at the top.
But they did not know what I meant, so they shut off the line,
And I was definitely not at all near fine.

I was standing there sad and gloomy
All hungry, ready for tea.
Then I looked up above, there was a man on the top,
He'd come to save me, and I felt my heart stop!

Now I'm safe, safe and sound.
And my mind is not spinning around.
But I'd like to say, 'just beware,'
Because one day elevators might give *you* a scare!

Melissa Bett (10)
Stickney CE Primary School

The Four Seasons

First comes spring, a new year's begun,
Children playing, having fun,
Animals come out again,
Waiting indoors for the rain,
Flowers begin to open up,
Daffodils and the buttercup.

Next comes summer after springtime,
Everybody eating lime,
People playing in the sea,
Picking flowers from a bee,
People walking in the breezy air,
Children playing on the fair.

Then comes autumn, time to wrap up,
It's time to have a lovely cup
Of hot chocolate, have a drink,
And some people like to think,
The leaves start to fall off the trees,
People's hats fly off in the breeze.

Last comes winter, snow starts to fall,
Blustery winds are winter's call,
The children play some snow games,
Children calling their friends names,
Children running round like fools,
Workmen leave out some rusty tools.

Now all these four seasons have gone,
We'll have to start another one,
Of these lovely special years,
Now don't worry of your fears,
Time to celebrate the seasons,
This poem has lots of reasons.

Natasha Corbitt (10)
Stickney CE Primary School

The Balloon's Journey

I am a balloon,
I am scrunched in a packet,
I'm just like the moon,
You must believe me, please, please!

I am a balloon,
And I have just been blown up,
I'm with a baboon,
You must believe me, please, please!

I am a balloon,
I am slowly floating up,
I'll reach the sky soon,
You must believe me, please, please!

I am a balloon,
I'm so high above the clouds,
I can see the moon,
You must believe me, please, please!

I am a balloon,
My eyes are being dazzled,
Because of the moon,
You must believe me, please, please!

I am a balloon,
I am slowly going down,
I will be flat soon,
You must believe me, please, please!

I am a balloon,
I died and floated to earth,
That's where I rested.

Roxanne Lenton (11)
Stickney CE Primary School

What Is . . . ?

What is orange? The sun is orange,
Bright and high in the sky.
What is red? Poppies are red,
Blowing seeds all around.
What is blue? The sky is blue,
Full of big, white planes.

What is green? Leaves are green,
Falling from trees so tall.
What is brown? Soil is brown,
All moist and wet with dew.
What is white? Daisies are white,
All trampled down by humans.

What is yellow? Sunflowers are yellow,
Standing tall and proud.
What is black? The sky is black,
All twinkling up with stars.
What is bright? The world is bright,
Full of glorious people.

Natasha Mitchell (10)
Stickney CE Primary School

Accidents Happen

On last week's school trip,
Joanna cut her lip,
The teacher said, 'Don't worry,
We will get your mum in a hurry.'

Her mum came in a hurry,
Saying don't you worry.
She threw her in the back,
With her brother Mac.

The next day was a scare,
When Hannah broke a chair.
The teacher got the glue,
Which was also blue.

At six o'clock was an alarm,
When Melissa broke her arm,
They called 999,
And got the class in a line,
That's what happened on last week's school trip.

Emily Dodds (10)
Stickney CE Primary School

The Old And Creaky Manor

The very old and creaky manor,
Stood there since I was born,
With its tales of haunting and dread,
So many people have stood to mourn.

With its worm-infested doors
And old and dusty floors,
The old and very creaky manor,
But it's still standing, so very demanding.

Every time you walk up and down,
The never-ending corridors,
Floorboards creak underneath your feet,
But it's still standing, so very demanding.

The people who lived there before,
Were haunted by the wicked ghosts,
They used to run away and hide,
But it's still standing, so very demanding.

Many people visit there every year,
With tales of old and grimy tears,
So many people have stood and stared,
But it's still standing, so very demanding.

Nadine Motley (11)
Stickney CE Primary School

I Went To The Future

I went to the future,
And guess what I saw?
I saw some singers,
So I shouted for more.

They sang, 'Hey, hey . . . '
And shouted, 'Doo, doo . . . '
I said, 'What are they?'
A woman said, 'They're new.'

So then I carried on,
And guess what I saw?
Everyone had gone,
So I went through a door.

The door spoke to me,
It said, 'You went to the future,
And guess what I saw?
I saw you coming through a wide open door.'

When it said that,
I was so amazed.
Then I saw a cat,
So it ran away for days.

Merrick Shaw (10)
Stickney CE Primary School

Space Flight

Flying through the moonlit sky,
Not caring where or why.

Waiting for a place to hit,
Falling rocks fall to bits!

Smashing through the starry night,
Flying way higher than a kite.

Whizzing past planets and the sun,
Having lots and lots of fun!

Lots of stardust in tow,
Smashing comets as I go.

Waiting for a place to dock,
I'll give people a great big shock!

Even though there is a lot of sorrow,
I'll fly again, maybe tomorrow!

Casey Jee (10)
Stickney CE Primary School

Protractor Boy

Protractor boy, protractor boy,
He's cool, he's smart,
Protractor boy, protractor boy,
His favourite food is custard tart.

Protractor boy, protractor boy,
His goldfish's named Bob,
Protractor boy, protractor boy,
His favourite poem's 'Doorknobs'.

Protractor boy, protractor boy,
He's mad on dinner ladies,
Protractor boy, protractor boy,
His favourite car is Mercedes.

Protractor boy, protractor boy,
He loves to swim but always ends up in the bin!

Sinead Holland (11)
Stickney CE Primary School

I Wasn't There When I Died!

I wasn't there when I died,
I went to bed to rest my head,
And my soul went free,
You must believe me.

I wasn't there when I died,
I had an out of body experience,
I went out of my own world or place,
And I saw a friendly face.

I wasn't there when I died,
I came back to my body,
It was beaten and battered,
You can see that I was shattered.

I wasn't there when I died,
My body's been found.
Police are investigating my death,
I want to tell them, but I have no breath.

I wasn't there when I died,
I don't know who killed me.
Whoever did, I will find out,
Until then, I'll float about.

I wasn't there when I died,
I can see the world go by,
I'm afraid and alone.
All I want is to go home.

I wasn't there when I died,
At home they are all grieving,
My wife and daughter Primrose,
How do I tell her I'm here, body and toes?

Francesca Warder (10)
Stickney CE Primary School

Me And My Dog

I've got a dog,
I go with it for walks,
So that I can jog.

That day I saw a frog,
Sitting on a big, brown log.

The next day I couldn't see because of the fog,
We carried on walking and we tripped over that log,
We could hear the frog,
The dog jumped up and started to jog.

'Slow down you silly dog!'
He stopped and barked when he saw a smelly hog.

The next day we went to the park,
My dog barked.
But guess what he saw?
It was the frog,
The frog had run under a big, brown log.

Rosemarie Holmes (11)
Stickney CE Primary School

Winter To Spring

Winter is as cold as a refrigerator.
Icicles are like the teeth of a sabre-toothed tiger
Hanging from a windowpane.
Rain is like a glitter tub upside down.
Ice like a brick wall, flat and hard.
An iceberg is like a house, but in the water.

Spring is warm as a cake on a plate.
Little flowers like a spring bouncing up and down.
Bunnies like little clouds on the ground.
Lambs like gas in the air.

Liam Greaves (9)
The Earl of Dysart Primary School

Poppies

Those little red flowers,
remind us of our sorrow,
tears come in showers,
as we pray for a better tomorrow.

Those little red flowers,
stand proud in the field,
tears come in showers,
as we remember the evil men yield.

Those little red flowers,
are a symbol of hope,
tears come in showers,
and help us to cope.

Those little red flowers,
remind us of our sorrow,
tears come in showers,
as we pray for a better tomorrow.

Lauren Towle (10)
The Earl of Dysart Primary School

Winter To Spring

The season of winter is as cold as the North Pole.
Icicles are as clear as a window.
In winter it is as white as a plain piece of paper.
Robins come in winter with their bright red tummies
that are as red as a stuffed nose with a cold.
When it snows the snow is like white feathers.

The season of spring reminds me of little baby animals being born.
The daffodils are popping up out of the ground like a spring.
Spring reminds me of a new life and the bright green fields.
In spring it is nice because the days last longer
like a clock going slower and slower.

Kayleigh Otter (10)
The Earl of Dysart Primary School

Winter To Spring

Winter
Winter is as cold as your refrigerator,
Icicles melt when they go near your radiator.
When people go outside they get frostbite,
But watch out, you might walk into a snowball fight.
Ice is as skiddy as roller-skates,
Sometimes people eat snow on plates.
You'll get very cold,
But you won't when you get old.
The blue sky goes away when it is fed on by the grey,
Just like an owl's prey.

Spring
Spring is warm,
It is when all the flowers come.
The leaves grow once again,
From the little buds they started as.
In spring it starts to get warmer,
But a bit breezy.
There are a few showers of rain,
But everyone is happy.

Calum McGhee (9)
The Earl of Dysart Primary School

Winter To Spring

Icicles hang sharp and sheer
makes you look white and clear.

Makes you cold and sore
after a while you get poor.

Snow is so crunchy like plastic
and is so, so, so, *so* fantastic.

Chaunie Dolby (9)
The Earl of Dysart Primary School

Winter To Spring

The winter season is as cold as the North Pole,
Icicles hang sharp and sheer, while the robins sing loud and clear.
Snow is falling like the rain in Noah's Ark,
Children play and make pearl-white snowmen.
Reindeer clip and clop at Christmas Eve,
Father Christmas brings nice and fun presents.
All the frost is turning to ice, so children think that's great,
Stockings hang from the warm, cosy fireplace.
Children are happy at all times and are having fun,
Everybody is making snow angels in the deep snow.
The North Star lights up the sky in the night,
Angels are singing to praise Jesus.
Sparkling ice is slippery and really cold.
But as the days grow old of the winter season,
Spring begins to move into the earth.
Lambs begin to be born, to open their eyes for the very first time,
A new life has just then begun.
Daffodils and snowdrops are appearing up from the ground,
Easter eggs are filling the shops as Easter is coming.
Bells are ringing from lambkins' collars,
Bunnies are hopping around the field.
But summer is coming soon.

Toni Freestone (9)
The Earl of Dysart Primary School

Winter To Spring

The season of winter is probably as cold as the North Pole.
Icicles get sharp and spiky, like on top of some fences.
Snow is like walking on people's bodies and breaking their bones.
It is freezing all around and it stays on my face like an ice-pack on
my face.

Kirsty Collin (10)
The Earl of Dysart Primary School

Winter To Spring

Winter
Winter is as cold as a refrigerator,
Winter is as cold as frozen peas,
Icicles are as sharp as dragon's teeth,
Snow is as fat as boulders,
Frozen lakes are like an ice-skating arena,
Snowballs are as round as an elephant's belly,
Icebergs are huge like a rhinoceros.

Spring
Beautiful newborn lambs,
Easter comes and you eat lots of chocolate,
Starting to get warmer like burning fires,
Blossoms starting to grow like other animals being born,
Leaves growing slow like a tortoise walking.

Aiden Wood (10)
The Earl of Dysart Primary School

Winter To Spring

Winter
The snow is cold as a refrigerator
Icicles are sharp and sheer, make our windows
Clear with freezing snowflakes falling on top
The sound of snowflakes every day
We hear the snowflakes falling on the winterly window
Soon it will be Christmas, it is fun on Christmas Day
When we go outside and play in the snow.

Spring
Spring is beautiful when the flowers and leaves
Go different colours, it goes warm at night
And bright in springtimes
I love spring because it is beautiful and fun.

Sophie Mudie (9)
The Earl of Dysart Primary School

Winter To Spring

Winter
The winter wind is as cold as a refrigerator.
The snow is pure white with grey patches and is freezing.
The snow is piled up and children run around playing and shouting.
People are all wrapped up in woollen clothes.
The ponds and rivers and streams are all icy and frozen.
The freezing cold wind is all blustery.
Children building snowmen in their gardens and throwing snowballs
at each other.
Icicles hanging from the bridge all sharp and pointed.
The sky is all dull and cloudy.

Spring
The cold air has turned warm and the flowers are blooming all around.
Leaves are growing on trees and grass is growing back.
The dull sky has turned a pure blue and is cloudless and new animals
are born.

Jamie Lawson (9)
The Earl of Dysart Primary School

Winter And Spring

Winter
The winter months are as cold as an ice pack.
Icicles are as sharp as a sabre-tooth tiger's.
I am as cold as an icicle.
It is raining cats and dogs today.
I like snow when it comes because you can have snowball fights.
My gloves are as warm as a summer's day.
My hat is too big for me and it falls over my head.
My big scarf is brilliant.

Spring
The grass is green and bright so everyone can look at it.
We will have a long night tonight
Because it is spring.
The farmer said, 'I just had a lamb born.'

Conor Bowen (10)
The Earl of Dysart Primary School

Winter To Spring

The season of winter is as cold as the North Pole
And as cold as a freezer, plus
Prickly icicles hang from your windowpane.

The slippery ice is slippery, dippery, you won't be able to walk
You'll spin forever and ever, plus
You won't be able to stop. Tea doesn't matter anymore.

New life makes me five years younger, it makes me more
Daring, plus caring, I'll be king of the world.

If you're frozen you'll be going knock, knock and knock again,
You'll be needing plutonium bombs to get yourself out!

Spring is relaxing, so lean back, eat some chocolate and
Drink hot cocoa, it'll hit the spot.

Brandon Duffield (9)
The Earl of Dysart Primary School

Winter

The season to be glad of
Is the season you will love
And the season you will love is winter.
Icicles hang sharp
With each on a blue mark
The skies grow heavy
As we take it steady.

Toni Morton (10)
The Earl of Dysart Primary School

Winter To Spring

Winter
The season of winter, it's as cold as ice, a fridge, the North Pole,
Like a bag of frozen peas on your cheek, and you get cold.
Icicles are sharp and sheer, as sharp as a sabre-toothed tiger's
tooth,
Snow makes your feet and fingers glow.

Spring
The season of spring is warm, new life is made, lambs are born,
Flowers bloom and the leaves come to the trees.
The wind is breezy, the grass grows for the new animals to eat,
Everyone's happy, the night becomes lighter by the minute than
winter.

Daniel Eve (10)
The Earl of Dysart Primary School

Winter To Spring

Winter is as cold as a bag of frozen peas,
Snow is like the icing of a cake that's been in a fridge for a year,
The frost is crunchy and sparkles like gems,
Christmas is the best day of the year,
Ice is sharp, thin and it glows like a fair,
Every person is wearing multicoloured warm scarves,
Gloves are attached to cold and icy hands.

Flowers bloom like a volcano eruption,
Newborn lambs and rabbits spring across the fields,
A new life is born,
Easter eggs and lots of other chocolate things,
From cold into a warm breeze,
Buds on the trees turning into a fresh green leaf.

Alex Harrold (9)
The Earl of Dysart Primary School

Romeo

The king of the cats comes down the street
Ready for his midnight treat.
His coat is black
His stripes are white
He never spoils a meal at night.

In the day he looks for girls
Seducing them with gold and pearls.
The king of the cats never sleeps
He's always ready to pounce and leap.
Romeo is very loud
Nevertheless he's forever proud.

He is the king of animal slaying
There's never time for him to be playing.
Romeo is a skinny cat
But when he gets older he could be quite fat.
Romeo will never die
And some people think he won't hurt a fly.

Henry Cliffe (10)
The Richmond School

Maria Muncher

Maria Muncher is a cunning kitty,
She attracts all the toms as she struts down the city,
She will never be ugly, she is always beautiful,
She's very sneaky and forever careful.

Maria is a glamorous cat,
She's dazzling white, now how about that?
She's a charming face and moonlit eyes,
But sometimes is sneaky and lies.

Maria Muncher has a furry tail,
But sometimes she gets a little bit pale,
When she is ill she looks after herself,
She makes herself comfy, she sleeps on the shelf.

Hannah Muirhead (9)
The Richmond School

A Christmas Dream For A Child In Africa

I don't get pressies,
Don't have a feast,
You must think,
I'm some kind of beast.

Don't go to bed early,
Don't wait for Santa to come,
Don't get kissed under the mistletoe,
Don't have fun.

We haven't got money,
To buy people gifts,
To get to Christmas parties,
We can't give them lifts.

But in my dream,
My African dream,
Christmas will come,
Just as it should seem.

Grace Phelps (10)
The Richmond School

Glamourpus

Glamourpus is a beautiful cat
She attracts all the boys, well fancy that!
Glamourpus is an amazing cool kitty
The boys stop to look as she struts down the city.

Glamourpus has snow-white fur
She has got an endearing purr
Glamourpus has incredible taste
But when it comes to restaurants, she stuffs her face.

Glamourpus does exercise and keeps very fit
She is a very cool cat and has a trendy kit
Glamourpus has a lot of friends
If they ever fall out, she always makes amends.

Sophie Gorrick (10)
The Richmond School

Montainiar

Montainiar is an intelligent cat,
She adores her inviting, snuggly mat,
Her brown and black coat is very tasteful,
She is still young and very graceful,
She's always in, never out,
She's never asleep, but always about.

Montainiar is a rather fussy eater,
She's definitely not a good sleeper,
If you call her, she's constantly there,
But of course she doesn't really care,
This charming cat likes to impress,
You'll never find her in a mess.

Montainiar's never walking, always at a run,
Forever looking up at the golden sun,
She likes to travel on a boat,
She'll look at others and sit and gloat,
She doesn't like to play hide-and-seek,
Before she snuggles down to sleep.

Bobbi Stead (10)
The Richmond School

Mifle

Mifle loves to be entertained,
She never goes out when she knows it has rained,
Her eyes so gold will shimmer in sun,
She always loves a bit of fun,
She messes around with a ball of wool,
Be careful though, cos she might pull.

Mifle likes to kill a mouse,
But then she likes to mess up the house,
She always is partial to a bit of meat,
But then again it's only a treat,
She loves it when somebody gives her a pat,
But when she is tired she sleeps on a mat.

Mifle sits on the warm, cosy chair,
And smiles at her friend, who lives near the fair,
Her fur so dark is as black as coal,
When she is itchy she rubs against the pole,
She is so small and as light as a feather,
She really is the best cat ever.

Lucie Millitt (9)
The Richmond School

Chocolate Chip

Chocolate Chip is astonishing,
He likes to wear his famous ring,
It's made of diamond, ruby and gold,
He's very gallant, strong and bold,
His fur is ebony and his eyes are green,
His coat is the sleekest you've ever seen.

Chocolate Chip will beat the rat,
He likes to sleep on a crimson mat,
He wears a suit, it's aquarium-blue,
He puts on his smart golden shoes,
As he walks along the royal, red mat,
Waiting for the trophy of the bestest cat.

Chocolate Chip gets on to the stage,
And there was the trophy, gold and beige,
He takes it off to his house,
Whilst enjoying a chocolate mouse,
And polishing his award with joy,
And playing with his favourite cat toy.

Jake Epton (9)
The Richmond School

Sabrinade

Sabrinade is a graceful dancer,
She is a long, powerful prancer,
All the cats treat her like the queen,
She hates all the things that are sneaky or mean,
Her favourite spot is sat by the fire,
She once had a friend who was a liar.

Sabrinade's a clever, intelligent cat,
She's not one that likes to see a bat,
Her tail is beautiful snow-white,
She has never in her life been in a fight,
In her luxury world she will sit,
She even has her very own sports kit.

Sabrinade is a Yorkshire puss,
She once leapt on a round the city bus,
In cat races she never comes last,
For she is really, really fast,
When she was younger she went to lessons of Latin,
She also was able to let any other cat in.

Rebecca Cram (9)
The Richmond School

Patch

Patch is a very strange cat
Everyone should know about that.
He really is a cunning fighter
He also is a dangerous biter.

Patch goes in a very bad mood
When he can't catch some food.
He always wants to eat some fish
He sometimes eats in a dish.

When he starts to chase a mouse
He'll accidentally wreck a house.
You'll always see him eat a rat
He'll keep on doing it till he gets fat.

Patch will get in lots of fights
There's lots of scratches, lots of bites.
He has a scratch across his back
His main foe is called Jack.

There's lots of patches on his face
He wishes to fly in outer space.
He really is a curious cat
Now everyone should know about that.

Brett Mason (10)
The Richmond School

Sneekerstock

Sneekerstock is tabby-coated,
She particularly likes to bounce,
She has a sister, Moonbeam's the name,
Who loves to catch a mouse,

Both of them are master criminals,
The pair are mysterious walkers,
Those two are deadly annihilators,
They are also secret talkers,

They sometimes amuse each other,
And they're always occupied,
They smash things and they steal things,
But never get in a fight,

Nevertheless they sometimes get caught,
'Cause they never have time to hide,
Their cousins don't even like them,
Of them they are petrified,

They will be eternally criminals,
They dwell in a reeking bin,
They're never going to be intelligent,
And they have committed lots of sin.

Bryony Hawkesford (10)
The Richmond School

Javillia

Javillia is a terrifying cat,
Who's constantly going for a rat,
She's always outside in the alley,
Fighting with her worst enemy Sally,
She's forever getting nasty mail,
And then being sent to jail.

Javillia only sleeps on a mat,
But always exterminating other cats,
She doesn't walk, only run,
And she's always looking up at the sun,
You don't want to get too close to her,
Else you will be facing a mouth full of fur.

Javillia stays in the pub all night,
And then goes to bed when it's light,
Javillia has got no chums,
To play with her when the work is done,
If you call her she's never there,
And of course she doesn't really care,
When it's late she goes to sleep,
But first she plays hide and go peep.

Sarah Beal (10)
The Richmond School

Masquerade The Mystic Cat

Masquerade - he's forever an illusion,
Wherever he is there is always confusion,
His amazing act of strange levitation,
Is famous across the entire nation.

Masquerade's face will remain unknown,
For no one has viewed him while he is alone,
One swirl of his cloak, you'll be surprised,
He'll vanish before your very eyes!

Masquerade then turns up on the chair -
Then you will see him on the stair!
His coat is chocolate, ebony and ginger,
One part of his coat is white - his finger.

Masquerade stalks the street at night,
Avoiding cats who like to fight,
In the day he will disappear,
Though you know he is somewhere near . . .

I've told you about Masquerade,
The cat who is always in the shade,
I've told you enough, and that is that!
Enough about Masquerade - the Mystic Cat!

Callum Dewar (10)
The Richmond School

NUFC

Our kit is so cool,
Black and white stripes,
Northern Rock the sponsor,
That's Sir Bobby's type.

Laurent Robert on the left,
Scoring all the screamers,
And there's Dyer down the centre,
Weaving all the wonders.

Aaron Hughes at the back,
Intercepting their attack,
Jonathan Woodgate helping out,
Gets the ball no doubt.

We're on the attack and getting nearer,
It's a *goal* from Alan Shearer.

Alex Pycock (10)
Tower Road Primary School

Snow

I woke up this morning, there was a nice surprise.
I opened the curtains, I couldn't believe my eyes.
When I went to school, my nose was rather stuffy.
And I was covered with snow that was very fluffy.
I like the snow, the snow is fun.
But when it melts, it's because of the sun.
There's no more snow for us to play.
And it was the end of the day.
From the snow I'd like to make a den.
Then on the next day it happened again.
I was very tired because I'm a sleepyhead.
But I had to go to school so I got out of bed.

Finn Lewis (9)
Tower Road Primary School

The Bird Poem

Birds, birds, I'm watching them fly,
Over the sea and over the sky.
They swoop low and they fly high,
Sliding by the blossom tree, I do wonder why.

Birds, birds, pecking on the ground,
Oh look, a worm, that's what they've found.
Then they fly away with the worm in their beaks,
While the cat looks up for a little sneaky peek.

Birds, birds, as pretty as you can be,
Swirl and twirl around the tree.
Birds, flying and flapping their wings,
Through the sky and upon the things.

Birds, birds, I'm watching them fly,
Over the sea and over the sky,
They swoop low and they fly high,
Sliding by the blossom tree, I do wonder why.

Sadia Aslam (9)
Tower Road Primary School

My Rugby Team

They're a . . .
Fast running
Ball smacking
Rugby thrashing
Neck breaking
Ball running
Head wacking
Nose bleeding
Rugby trying
Top score making
Sort of team.

Alistair Wood (10)
Tower Road Primary School

Billy Attacked The Teacher!

It was our last PE lesson,
We were playing volleyball,
When Bill threw the ball at the teacher
And she wasn't happy at all.

Her face went as red as a rose,
Smoke gushed out of her ears,
She started advancing on Billy
And that was the worst of his fears.

His face went as pale as pale,
Tears filled his eyes,
He cowered in his teacher's wake
Then burst into loud, noisy cries.

'I'm really sorry,
I didn't mean to aim for you,
I meant to hit it over
Forgive me, please do!'

Note: Never stand near a teacher
When you're playing ball games.

Charlotte Doddrell (10)
Tower Road Primary School

White Snow

The sun is shining on the snow,
The wind is really trying to blow.
Children's feet,
Really need some heat.
Some children's hair,
Is blowing in the air.
The powdery snow is ready to blow,
All of this in the snow.

Michael Craven (8)
Tower Road Primary School

The Lonely Family

When my father went out to war
I was very, very, very distraught.
His stocking hangs upon the place
Under the tree his presents lay.

I say, 'Daddy's gone for a few days,'
I only wish it really was a few days.
The house is empty without him here
My heart feels lonely while he's gone.

I remember the days that we had
Playing in the park, riding a boat.
So now you know how we feel
We continue with our life . . .
Just as normal.

Katie Toyne (11)
Tower Road Primary School

Magical Sadness

A unicorn is lovely
It's my favourite thing
But I am not one
Which is really annoying

I love the way the dragon
Breathes fire to keep him snug
But I can't breathe fire
I always need a rug

I wish I was magical
It makes me feel sad
To think that they are magical
While all I am is mad!

Lucy Doddrell (8)
Tower Road Primary School

The Calindarats

In the shadows
Where the dwelling
Somewhere no one knows
Is a merchant telling
His old story
From the past
Full of glory
That could never last

It all started
One dark night
Where his goods were carted.
From the darkness emerged a knight
He said he sought
The lair of the Calindarats
He needed to be caught
And sent to the prison near the Atts

The Atts are in
The mountainside
Of the great Klin
Where the two continents divide.
A year later
On his journey back
As he travelled through nature
In a great big sack
The knight had the Calindarats.

Aidan McClure (10)
Tower Road Primary School

My Sister

I have a little sister,
Who's always in a blister,
And all she does is cry,
Which makes my clever brain fry,
I hope to God she grows up fast,
So I can have some peace at last.

Mehroz Waheed (9)
Tower Road Primary School

Writing A Poem

I want to write a poem
But I don't know what to write
Shall I write about a great big bird
Flying, flying out of sight?

Or shall I write about a fish
Gliding through the ocean blue
And what about the green, green trees?
I don't know what to do!

Could I write one really long
Or shall I keep it small?
How about some princesses
Looking lovely at a ball?

Now I'm feeling quite confused
Should it rhyme or should it not?
Or shall I just forget it now?
I've thought of quite a lot.

I think I'll just give up right now
I'm starting to feel cross
Actually I have no choice
Cos really Mum's the boss.

Aafreen Shaikh (11)
Tower Road Primary School

The Snow Today

The snow today is very cold,
It tries to freeze my feet,
The snow today is falling still, so I was told,
It will make a great big treat!
The snow today is not a very good mould,
Now here I am trying to find a seat.

Ella Dodd (9)
Tower Road Primary School

Pirates

I was all alone, stranded at sea,
When a ship started sailing over to me.
The great galleon sparked my greatest fear,
What if its inhabitants had been dead for years?
The ship got closer, I could feel the chill,
The waves got rough, so rough until,
The galloon stopped, extremely close,
And from the ship, ebony shadows rose.
I watched the sight as the shapes got closer,
I watched, as the faces became somewhat grosser.
They were now inches from my face,
I could not identify their nature or race.
One had scars covering his arm,
One had remarkably not come to any harm.
One looked like he was plagued of thirst,
But their leader, their captain, was by far the worst.
This man was not short nor indeed thin,
None of them looked like his immediate kin.
This monster stood towering over them all,
Very heavy and exceptionally tall.
He said, 'Ahoy, me hearties,' in the most roughest tone,
'We are tekkin' o'er this land,' in much more of a drone.
The pirates came in with treasure and attire,
And their first instinct was to start a fire.
Burning the island as they went,
Burning the trees with no consent.
I watched as the island transformed to ashes,
I looked at my arm; it was covered in slashes.
I slowly turned and there he stood,
A knife in his hand, his hands covered in blood.

Joe Roper (11)
Tower Road Primary School

Karry And Mary

Karry and Mary
Slept in a shell;
Sleep, little child!
And they slept well.

Blue was the shell within,
Silver without;
Sounds of the bright sea
Wandered about.

Sleep, little child,
Wake not soon!
Dream on dream
Dies to the moon.

Two yellow stars
Peeped into the shell;
'What are they dreaming of,
Who can tell?'

Startled a green bird
Out of the croft;
'Wake, little child,
The sun is aloft!'

Karry and Mary
Wake up from a dream,
Had a yawn as if they had eaten,
Smell of food, 'I wonder what
Mother has cooked?
Fish.' Yum-yum!

They ate and said,
'Will we sleep in that shell again?'
Mother said to them,
'Yes, but right now, let's play a game!'

Hanna Zafar (9)
Tower Road Primary School

Out In The Street

Out in the street I went for a treat,
Down in the gutters the mice all squeak,
Out of one eye I saw someone peek,
While me and my sister play hide and seek.

Out in the street the dogs all bark,
While me and my mates played tig in the park,
One of my mate's name is called Mark,
While my sister plays with her dog named Clark.

Out in the street I heard a tap,
Some of my mates have bought a new cap,
Sometime this week I bought a new map
That is the end of my groovy little rap.

Natasha Lenton (9)
Tower Road Primary School

I Wake Up

I wake up,
I am bodyless,
I can't feel my arms,
I can't feel my legs,
I can't feel my nose.

I can't feel my mouth,
I can't feel my hair,
I can't feel my toes,
I can't feel my ears,
I can't feel me!
So I am going to go to sleep again!

Lindsay Atkinson (9)
Tower Road Primary School

My Rap
(Inspired by 'Gran Can You Rap?' by Jack Ousbey)

As they walked in the room
they danced till noon,
I heard a bin ban boom
and there was the moon.
I'm the best rapping kid this world's ever seen
I'm a zigzag, zip-zap, rap rap queen.

As I picked up a rose
I did a cool pose,
and my best friend Kia
drank all my beer.
I'm the best rapping kid this world's ever seen
I'm a tic-tac, tick-tock, rap rap queen.

As I walked down the street
I kept tapping my feet to the beat,
I know I can dance
to the rhythm of the beat.
I'm the best rapping kid this world's ever seen
I'm a
zigzag,
zip-zap,
tic-tac,
tick-tock,
chit-chat,
take a sleep,
have a peep,
happy, happy, happy, happy,
rap rap queen.

Adelaide Esdale (8)
Weston Hills CE Primary School

The Winter Birds

I look out of the window
I see the snow
High up in the trees
The birds always go.

I look at the ground
And what do I see,
Footprints in the snow
From birds in the tree.

When the snow starts to melt
The footprints do too
The birds start to sing
To me and you!

Demi Powell (9)
Weston Hills CE Primary School

Maths

M aths is a subject I really enjoy
A lways I do maths with my brother Roy
T wenty-two problems to solve, every day
H ow do you do it? That's not what I say!
S leepy, my brain, after all this maths.
   Please go to bed at the end of this task!

Kate Harwood (9)
Weston Hills CE Primary School

Tigor, Tigor
(Based on 'The Tiger' by William Blake)

Tiger, tiger in the night
Prowling round just for a fight
Watching, staring at the deer
Stay away and run in fear

In the bushes there he is
He's killed a deer and thinks it's his
Guarding it with all his power
In every long and tiring hour

When he jumps up in the tree
Looking round and watching me
I wish I was home, safe in bed
In case he gets me; then I'm dead.

Jacob Read (9)
Weston Hills CE Primary School

Baby Elephant

Baby elephant left alone
Mother killed for her ivory bone,
Poor baby elephant abandoned accidentally
Put in Born Free, who are kind and friendly,
Ready to be adopted with lots of hope and glee
Maybe one day she will be free.

Beth Turnell (9)
Weston Hills CE Primary School

My Kid's Rap
(Inspired by 'Gran Can You Rap?' by Jack Ousbey)

As I walked in the room
I saw my mum on a broom
I saw a ball
On top of the hall
I'm the best rapping kid this world's ever seen
I'm a kit-kat, flap-flip, rap rap queen

As I rolled down the hill
I saw an empty till
I saw Paul on top of a broken wall
I'm the best rapping kid this world's ever seen
I'm a zip-zap, zag-zag, rap rap queen

As I walked down the street
I was tapping my feet
I love to dance
To the rhythm of the beat
I'm the best rapping kid this world's ever seen
I'm a hip-hop, splat-split, rap rap queen.

Jade Gilbert (8)
Weston Hills CE Primary School